Table Of Contents

Topic	Page #
My Personal Testimony	3
You Must Participate In Your Own Miracle	5
You Can Only Conquer What You Hate	6
Your Greatest Weapon In The Battle For Your Healing	6
How To Use This Book To Receive Your Personal Healing	7
How To Use This Book To Help Others Receive Their Healing	9
Unleashing Healing Faith Through The Word Of God (407 Scriptures)	11
Your Healing Is A Harvest From A Loving God	72

un paged 74-76

Unless otherwise indicated, all Scripture quotations are taken from the King James Version of the Bible.
Passport to Health & Healing
ISBN 1-56394-367-0/B-271
Copyright © 2006 **MIKE MURDOCK**
All publishing rights belong exclusively to Wisdom International
Published by The Wisdom Center · 4051 Denton Hwy. · Ft. Worth, TX 76117
Publisher/Editor: Deborah Murdock Johnson
1-817-759-BOOK · 1-817-759-2665
You Will Love Our Website...! www.TheWisdomCenter.tv
Printed in the United States of America. All rights reserved under International Copyright Law. Contents and/or cover may not be reproduced in whole or in part in any form without the express written consent of the publisher.

The Word Of God
Within You
Is The Power Of God
Within You.

-MIKE MURDOCK

Copyright © 2005 by Mike Murdock • Wisdom International
The Wisdom Center • 4051 Denton Hwy. • Ft. Worth, TX 76117

My Personal Testimony

One Intercessor Can Change Your Life...Forever.

The first Turning-Point of my life took place when I was two-and-a-half years old...and I did not even know it.

All of my family has discussed this my entire life. I would encourage you to read my mother's book, *Dear Misty*. It contains a more thorough account.

Here is a summary of my first healing. When I was two-and-a-half years old, I was eaten up with worms. In fact, my mother decided to count the worms that came out of my body in a single day. Some even crawled out of my mouth on the shoulder of those holding me.

Over 600 worms in a single day.

For a season I even lost the ability to walk. My mother took me to two doctors. The conclusive diagnosis of both was that there was no known cure. One even stated, "He will die any day, and I don't want his death on my record." Medical doctors said that there was no hope of my recovery.

One night, my father decided to set aside the entire night to focus on praying for my healing. He has always been an Intercessor. (In fact, in 1953, he decided that he could accomplish more through prayer than through his preaching.) He made a Turning-Point decision in his own life..."to give himself to prayer." The Word declares that "Two are better than one," (Ecclesiastes 4:9). It is true that one person can put 1,000 to flight...but two will put ten thousand to flight!

The Power of Two.

Think about this. This why I am writing this book...to unlock the Rewards of Agreement for your personal healing. Satan never emerged in the Garden of Eden until Eve was created to walk by Adam's side.

Satan's greatest fear is...Relationships. Especially, any Divine Connection that births the perfect Will of God.

An extra word about my father. He is over 90 years old. He has prayed four to ten hours a day every day of his life...and has never been hospitalized for a day.

Back to my testimony: My father was determined to get an answer from God regarding my physical healing. He has stated about this, "I did not know exactly how to pray or what to pray for. I just wanted the Will of God done in his little body. But I had a strange peace that is hard to explain as I knelt to pray." As he knelt on his knees, he lifted his hands. But only one sentence began to come out of his lips. "Thou art a mighty God." Suddenly, that became the only sentence in his prayer as he began to repeat that statement over and over with a mental picture of me in his mind. Over and over, he prayed this sentence: "Thou art a mighty God! Thou art a mighty God! Thou art a mighty God!" Within a few moments he began to have a mental picture of Jesus walking over to where satan was holding me in his arms. My father explained it this way, "Jesus did not say anything to satan. There was no word spoken at all. It simply seemed that Jesus gently took your little body out of the arms of satan. I somehow knew God had answered my prayers and all was well."

The next morning I suddenly had a desire to eat and began to act normal.

I was miraculously healed.
One Intercessor changed my life forever.
There are some people God truly enjoys.
There are some people God favors.
There are some people God answers.

The power of one Intercessor in your life is immeasurable. Your miracle does not require 10,000 people praying for you. Your miracle simply requires one person in Agreement with you...for the Will of God to be done for your life.

Do you have anyone conversing with God about you? Do you have anyone presenting your Name, your Need, your legal case in the Courtroom of The Eternal Judge?

One Intercessor, who feels your pain, willing to enter the presence of God on your behalf, can silence the roar of 10,000 demon spirits assigned to sabotage you.

Yet, a strange phenomenon occurs every day in Christianity. Millions receive letters from preachers who want to pray for them. Prayer Request Forms are included so The Prayer Team can hold them before God in intercession. What is our reaction? Most Christians throw those Prayer Sheets into the trash can.

Every time you throw a Prayer Request Form into the trash can, you have lost another miracle.

You Must Participate In Your Own Miracle

You must *reach*.
You must *pursue*.
You must fight *back*.
Reaching is proof of Desire.

Reaching again and again...is proof of Passion. Reaching reveals humility and awareness of need. Reaching documents your confidence in God. Reaching is the Arrow of Faith targeted toward the Covenant we have with God.

Tolerance of your present disease breathes life into it. *Whatever You Can Tolerate You Cannot Change.* Endurance has its own rewards, but Change is not one of them. The unwillingness to accept your sickness unleashes the supernatural power of The Healer Whose presence is in you this very moment.

You Can Only Conquer What You Hate

Warfare Always Surrounds The Birth Of A Miracle. Earth is an adversarial environment. Spoils belong to Warriors.

The blind man cried out louder...when the crowd wanted him to stay silent. Do you remember the little woman who had an issue of blood for 12 years? Doctors had even given up. But, she did not give up on herself. She fought her way through the crowd to touch the hem of the garment of Jesus. *She received what she was willing to fight for.*

Do you have a spirit of a fighter?

Do you hate your disease?

Do you despise your pain?

Warriors qualify for Victory.

Your Greatest Weapon In The Battle For Your Healing

The love of God cannot be doubted. He gave His Son, Jesus, to save us from our sins. The Cross is proof of His Passion for our salvation. Yet, you cannot even experience salvation...until you decide to *believe*.

What is your greatest weapon? Your faith in God and the belief that He personally wants you healed.

How do you generate powerful and strong faith that defeats invisible disease and pain? "Faith comes by hearing...The Word of God." (See Romans 10:17.)

The Words of God are Seeds containing invisible Power, Healing and Authority. When His Words enter your spirit, strength grows like any Seed planted in soil. Your Mind-Garden has received (heard) many words of doubt that have grown...Weeds of Unbelief.

There is Hope.

Change can come.

Your healing is already beginning.

You can grow new Seed in your Mind-Garden. What is The Cure?

Faith-Seed.

Your hope is...to grow NEW Seed...in your Mind-Garden.

That is why I compiled these words for your healing. It is your turn for a miracle. The words of the famous songwriter, Stuart Hamlen, are so powerful.

"It is no secret what God can do.

What He's done for others, He will do for you."

I wrote a song many years ago, "He's A Healing Jesus." He is. Dare to believe it.

Your Future Is Decided By Who You Have Chosen To Believe.

How To Use This Book To Receive Your Personal Healing

1. Read The 7-Day Healing Calendar Aloud Three Times A Day. First, when you awaken each morning. Read it again before you eat your noon meal (12:00 pm). Read it again just before you turn off the light to go to sleep. Remember The Wisdom Key: *What You Keep Hearing You Eventually Believe.*

2. Memorize ONE Scripture-of-the-Day. It is Seed in your Mind-Garden...growing your Forest of Faith. These healing scriptures, create a new focus away from your pain and sickness. Remember The Wisdom Key: *Anything That Keeps Your Attention Has Become Your Master.*

3. Pray This Prayer Of Expectation When You Finish Reading Your Daily Healing Scriptures.

"Precious Father,

I love You with my whole heart. I am thankful for every good thing that has come from You. You are my Source, my Provider, my Deliverer and my Healer. That is why I serve You, trust You and approach You with boldness and great expectation of the miracle I need today.

I come to You in the powerful Name of Jesus of Nazareth, by Whose stripes I am healed. I take authority over all disease, all disorder, all pain and all sickness in my body. In the Name of Jesus, I command all pain and disease to leave my body now and forever. I am Your child, Your property, and Your temple where You abide and live as the Force of my life. I receive Your Word as Your Covenant with me for Divine health and Divine healing. I choose to believe that You are my Healer, my Deliverer, my Saviour and my King. Disease and sickness cannot reign nor rule in my body from this day forward. I declare and believe this both publicly and privately under the authority of the Name of Jesus. It is done. Amen."

4. Identify The Intercessors Who Are

Willing To Pray In Faith And Agreement With You For The Same Healing You Are Receiving. Agreement works. (Read Matthew 18:18-19 and decide to believe it.) Do not isolate yourself and withdraw from your Prayer Partners.

5. **Write Or Telephone The Prayer Center Here At Our Ministry So Our Intercessors Can Pray With You.** (The Prayer Center telephone number here is 817-838-PRAY.)

How To Use This Book To Help Others Receive Their Healing

1. **Decide To Be A Deliverer To Those In Captivity.** Someone needs you. What God has done for you must be shared with those experiencing a satanic attack on their personal health. You are the bridge to their miracle. Never forget this. Never assume that others already know what you know. Thousands have been taught that Jesus does not heal today. You can plant the Seed that grows their faith for their personal miracle. "...a faithful ambassador is health," (Proverbs 13:17).

2. **Schedule A Personal Appointment To Enter The Arena Of Their Health Battle.** Decide to become their golden link to the world of faith. Remember The Wisdom Key: *When God Wants To Bless You, He Sends A Person Into Your Life.* You must take action. You must reach...telephone them...visit them in the hospital...and decide to become The Sower of Faith Seed into their Mind-Garden.

3. **Sow This Book As Your Love-Seed.** It creates a memory of your visit of compassion. It proves your confidence that God will unleash a healing river into their life. This book can forever

change the Season of Pain into the Season of Joy.

   4. **Telephone Your Friend And Read The Daily Healing Calendar Aloud To Them.** Sometimes, we hurt too much to reach. They may need to access your faith, your voice and your caring. Do not preach to them. Do not criticize them like the comforters of Job who were so deadly in their words of advice. Simply read the Scriptures-of-the-Day to them...including The Healing Prayer.

*What You Make Happen For Others,
God Will Make Happen For You.*

   Your Prayer Partner,

   Mike Murdock

RECOMMENDED FOR YOUR WISDOM LIBRARY:
B-196 The Memory Bible on Healing (32 pages/$3)
B-197 The Memory Bible on Faith (32 pages/$3)

Unleashing Healing Faith Through The Word Of God

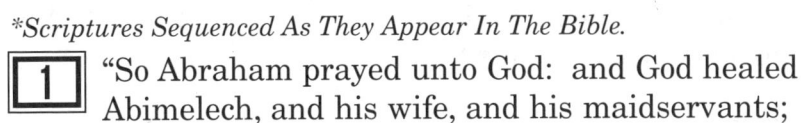

Scriptures Sequenced As They Appear In The Bible.

1. "So Abraham prayed unto God: and God healed Abimelech, and his wife, and his maidservants; and they bare children," (Genesis 20:17).

2. "And in very deed for this cause have I raised thee up, for to shew in thee My power; and that My name may be declared throughout all the earth," (Exodus 9:16).

3. "And it shall be when thy son asketh thee in time to come, saying, What is this? that thou shalt say unto him, By strength of hand the Lord brought us out from Egypt, from the house of bondage," (Exodus 13:14).

4. "The Lord shall fight for you, and ye shall hold your peace," (Exodus 14:14).

5. "The Lord is my strength and song, and He is become my salvation: He is my God, and I will prepare Him an habitation; my father's God, and I will exalt Him," (Exodus 15:2).

6. "And said, If thou wilt diligently hearken to the voice of the Lord thy God, and wilt do that which is right in His sight, and wilt give ear to His commandments, and keep all His statutes, I will put none of these diseases upon thee, which I have brought upon the Egyptians: for I am the Lord that healeth thee," (Exodus 15:26).

7 "But if thou shalt indeed obey His voice, and do all that I speak; then I will be an enemy unto thine enemies, and an adversary unto thine adversaries," (Exodus 23:22).

8 "And ye shall serve the Lord your God, and He shall bless thy bread, and thy water; and I will take sickness away from the midst of thee," (Exodus 23:25).

9 "By little and little I will drive them out from before thee, until thou be increased, and inherit the land," (Exodus 23:30).

10 "And He said, My presence shall go with thee, and I will give thee rest," (Exodus 33:14).

11 "The flesh also, in which, even in the skin thereof, was a boil, and is healed," (Leviticus 13:18).

12 "But I have said unto you, Ye shall inherit their land, and I will give it unto you to possess it, a land that floweth with milk and honey: I am the Lord your God, which have separated you from other people," (Leviticus 20:24).

13 "God is not a man, that He should lie; neither the son of man, that He should repent: hath He said, and shall He not do it? or hath He spoken, and shall He not make it good," (Numbers 23:19).

14 "Ye shall walk in all the ways which the Lord your God hath commanded you, that ye may live, and that it may be well with you, and that ye may prolong your days in the land which ye shall possess," (Deuteronomy 5:33).

15 "Hear therefore, O Israel, and observe to do it; that it may be well with thee, and that ye may increase mightily, as the Lord God of thy fathers hath promised thee, in the land that floweth with milk and honey," (Deuteronomy 6:3).

16 "And thou shalt do that which is right and good in the sight of the Lord: that it may be well with thee, and that thou mayest go in and possess the good land which the Lord sware unto thy fathers," (Deuteronomy 6:18).

17 "To cast out all thine enemies from before thee, as the Lord hath spoken," (Deuteronomy 6:19).

18 "And the Lord commanded us to do all these statutes, to fear the Lord our God, for our good always, that He might preserve us alive, as it is at this day," (Deuteronomy 6:24).

19 "Wherefore it shall come to pass, if ye hearken to these judgments, and keep, and do them, that the Lord thy God shall keep unto thee the covenant and the mercy which He sware unto thy fathers," (Deuteronomy 7:12).

20 "And He will love thee, and bless thee, and multiply thee: He will also bless the fruit of thy womb, and the fruit of thy land, thy corn, and thy wine, and thine oil, the increase of thy kine, and the flocks of thy sheep, in the land which He sware unto thy fathers to give thee," (Deuteronomy 7:13).

21 "Thou shalt be blessed above all people: there shall not be male or female barren among you, or among your cattle," (Deuteronomy 7:14).

22 "And the Lord will take away from thee all sickness, and will put none of the evil diseases of Egypt, which thou knowest, upon thee; but will lay them upon all them that hate thee," (Deuteronomy 7:15).

23 "For the Lord thy God bringeth thee into a good land, a land of brooks of water, of fountains and depths that spring out of valleys and hills," (Deuteronomy 8:7).

24 "A land of wheat, and barley, and vines, and fig trees, and pomegranates; a land of oil olive, and honey," (Deuteronomy 8:8).

25 "A land wherein thou shalt eat bread without scarceness, thou shalt not lack any thing in it; a land whose stones are iron, and out of whose hills thou mayest dig brass," (Deuteronomy 8:9).

26 "Keep therefore the words of this covenant, and do them, that ye may prosper in all that ye do," (Deuteronomy 29:9).

27 "See now that I, even I, am He, and there is no god with Me: I kill, and I make alive; I wound, and I heal: neither is there any that can deliver out of My hand," (Deuteronomy 32:39).

28 "Have not I commanded thee? Be strong and of a good courage; be not afraid, neither be thou dismayed: for the Lord thy God is with thee whithersoever thou goest," (Joshua 1:9).

29 "And they said, If ye send away the ark of the God of Israel, send it not empty; but in any wise return Him a trespass offering: then ye shall be healed, and it shall be known to you why His hand is not removed from you," (1 Samuel 6:3).

30 "Now therefore stand and see this great thing, which the Lord will do before your eyes," (1 Samuel 12:16).

31 "Let our lord now command thy servants, which are before thee, to seek out a man, who is a cunning player on an harp: and it shall come to pass, when the evil spirit from God is upon thee, that he shall play with his hand, and thou shalt be well," (1 Samuel 16:16).

32 "And it came to pass, when the evil spirit from God was upon Saul, that David took an harp, and played with his hand: so Saul was refreshed, and was well, and the evil spirit departed from him," (1 Samuel 16:23).

33 "He brought me forth also into a large place: He delivered me, because He delighted in me. For Thou art my lamp, O Lord: and the Lord will lighten my darkness. For by Thee I have run through a troop: by my God have I leaped over a wall," (2 Samuel 22:20, 29-30).

34 "God is my strength and power: and He maketh my way perfect," (2 Samuel 22:33).

35 "He teacheth my hands to war; so that a bow of steel is broken by mine arms," (2 Samuel 22:35).

36 "Blessed be the Lord, that hath given rest unto His people Israel, according to all that He promised: there hath not failed one word of all His good promise, which He promised by the hand of Moses His servant," (1 Kings 8:56).

37 "And he went forth unto the spring of the waters, and cast the salt in there, and said, Thus saith the Lord, I have healed these waters; there shall not be from thence any more death or barren land," (2 Kings 2:21).

38 "So the waters were healed unto this day, according to the saying of Elisha which he spake," (2 Kings 2:22).

39 "And the Lord was with him; and he prospered whithersoever he went forth: and he rebelled against the king of Assyria, and served him not," (2 Kings 18:7).

40 "Turn again, and tell Hezekiah the captain of My people, Thus saith the Lord, the God of David thy father, I have heard thy prayer, I have seen thy tears: behold, I will heal thee: on the third day thou shalt go up unto the house of the Lord," (2 Kings 20:5).

41 "Glory ye in His holy name: let the heart of them rejoice that seek the Lord," (1 Chronicles 16:10).

42 "Seek the Lord and His strength, seek His face continually," (1 Chronicles 16:11).

43 "Remember His marvellous works that He hath done, His wonders, and the judgments of His mouth," (1 Chronicles 16:12).

44 "Glory and honour are in His presence; strength and gladness are in His place," (1 Chronicles 16:27).

45 "And David said to Solomon his son, Be strong and of good courage, and do it: fear not, nor be dismayed: for the Lord God, even my God, will be with thee; He will not fail thee, nor forsake thee, until thou hast finished all the work for the service of the house of the Lord," (1 Chronicles 28:20).

46 "Both riches and honour come of Thee, and Thou reignest over all; and in Thine hand is power and might; and in Thine hand it is to make great, and to give strength unto all," (1 Chronicles 29:12).

47 "Now, my God, let, I beseech Thee, Thine eyes be open, and let Thine ears be attent unto the prayer that is made in this place," (2 Chronicles 6:40).

48 "If My people, which are called by My name, shall humble themselves, and pray, and seek My face, and turn from their wicked ways; then will I hear from heaven, and will forgive their sin, and will heal their land," (2 Chronicles 7:14).

49 "For the eyes of the Lord run to and fro throughout the whole earth, to shew Himself strong in the behalf of them whose heart is perfect toward Him. Herein thou hast done foolishly: therefore from henceforth thou shalt have wars," (2 Chronicles 16:9).

50 "My sons, be not now negligent: for the Lord hath chosen you to stand before Him, to serve Him, and that ye should minister unto Him, and burn incense. Then the Levites arose, Mahath the son of Amasai, and Joel the son of Azariah, of the sons of the Kohathites: and of the sons of Merari, Kish the son of Abdi, and Azariah the son of Jehalelel: and of the Gershonites; Joah the son of Zimmah, and Eden the son of Joah," (2 Chronicles 29:11-12).

51 "And the Lord hearkened to Hezekiah, and healed the people," (2 Chronicles 30:20).

52 "Then he said unto them, Go your way, eat the fat, and drink the sweet, and send portions unto them for whom nothing is prepared: for this day is holy unto our Lord: neither be ye sorry; for the joy of the Lord is your strength," (Nehemiah 8:10).

53 "Thy words have upholden him that was falling, and Thou hast strengthened the feeble knees," (Job 4:4).

54 "For He maketh sore, and bindeth up: He woundeth, and His hands make whole," (Job 5:18).

55 "Thou hast granted me life and favour, and Thy visitation hath preserved my spirit," (Job 10:12).

56 "Have pity upon me, have pity upon me, O ye my friends; for the hand of God hath touched me," (Job 19:21).

57 "Acquaint now thyself with Him, and be at peace: thereby good shall come unto thee," (Job 22:21).

58 "Thou shalt also decree a thing, and it shall be established unto thee: and the light shall shine upon thy ways," (Job 22:28).

59 "The Spirit of God hath made me, and the breath of the Almighty hath given me life," (Job 33:4).

60 "He will deliver his soul from going into the pit, and his life shall see the light. Lo, all these things worketh God oftentimes with man, To bring back his soul from the pit, to be enlightened with the light of the living," (Job 33:28-30).

61 "He withdraweth not His eyes from the righteous; but with kings are they on the throne: yea, He doth establish them for ever, and they are exalted," (Job 36:7).

62 "If they obey and serve Him, they shall spend their days in prosperity, and their years in pleasures," (Job 36:11).

63 "He delivereth the poor in His affliction and openeth their ears in oppression," (Job 36:15).

64 "Who hath enjoined Him his way? or who can say, Thou hast wrought iniquity?" (Job 36:23).

65 "Touching the Almighty, we cannot find Him out: He is excellent in power, and in judgment, and in plenty of justice: He will not afflict," (Job 37:23).

66 "I will both lay me down in peace, and sleep: for Thou, Lord, only makest me dwell in safety," (Psalm 4:8).

67 "The Lord hath heard my supplication; the Lord will receive my prayer," (Psalm 6:9).

68 "I have set the Lord always before me: because He is at my right hand, I shall not be moved.

Therefore my heart is glad, and my glory rejoiceth: my flesh also shall rest in hope," (Psalm 16:8-9).

69 "The Lord is my rock, and my fortress, and my deliverer; my God, my strength, in whom I will trust; my buckler, and the horn of my salvation, and my high tower," (Psalm 18:2).

70 "For Thou wilt light my candle: the Lord my God will enlighten my darkness. It is God that girdeth me with strength, and maketh my way perfect," (Psalm 18:28, 32).

71 "Now know I that the Lord saveth His anointed; He will hear him from His holy heaven with the saving strength of His right hand," (Psalm 20:6).

72 "Thou hast given him his heart's desire, and hast not withholden the request of his lips. He asked life of Thee, and Thou gavest it him, even length of days for ever and ever," (Psalm 21:2, 4).

73 "But be not Thou far from me, O Lord: O my strength, haste Thee to help me," (Psalm 22:19).

74 "For He hath not despised nor abhorred the affliction of the afflicted; neither hath He hid His face from him; but when he cried unto Him, He heard," (Psalm 22:24).

75 "Yea, though I walk through the valley of the shadow of death, I will fear no evil: for Thou art with me; Thy rod and Thy staff they comfort me," (Psalm 23:4).

76 "The Lord is my light and my salvation; whom shall I fear? the Lord is the strength of my life; of whom shall I be afraid?" (Psalm 27:1).

77 "One thing have I desired of the Lord, that will I seek after; that I may dwell in the house of the Lord all the days of my life, to behold the beauty of the Lord, and to enquire in His temple. For in the time of trouble He shall hide me in His pavilion: in the secret of His tabernacle shall He hide me; He shall set me up upon a rock," (Psalm 27:4-5).

78 "The Lord is my strength and my shield; my heart trusted in Him, and I am helped: therefore my heart greatly rejoiceth; and with my song will I praise Him," (Psalm 28:7).

79 "The Lord is their strength, and He is the saving strength of His anointed," (Psalm 28:8).

80 "The Lord will give strength unto His people; the Lord will bless His people with peace," (Psalm 29:11).

81 "O Lord my God, I cried unto Thee, and Thou hast healed me," (Psalm 30:2).

82 "...weeping may endure for a night, but joy cometh in the morning," (Psalm 30:5).

83 "O love the Lord, all ye His saints: for the Lord preserveth the faithful, and plentifully rewardeth the proud doer," (Psalm 31:23).

84 "Be of good courage, and He shall strengthen your heart, all ye that hope in the Lord," (Psalm 31:24).

85 "Thou art my hiding place; Thou shalt preserve me from trouble; Thou shalt compass me about with songs of deliverance," (Psalm 32:7).

86 "Behold, the eye of the Lord is upon them that fear Him, upon them that hope in His mercy; To deliver their soul from death, and to keep them alive in famine," (Psalm 33:18-19).

87 "I sought the Lord, and He heard me, and delivered me from all my fears," (Psalm 34:4).

88 "The angel of the Lord encampeth round about them that fear Him, and delivereth them," (Psalm 34:7).

89 "The eyes of the Lord are upon the righteous, and His ears are open unto their cry. The righteous cry, and the Lord heareth, and delivereth them out of all their troubles," (Psalm 34:15, 17).

90 "Many are the afflictions of the righteous: but the Lord delivereth him out of them all," (Psalm 34:19).

91 "Delight thyself also in the Lord; and He shall give thee the desires of thine heart," (Psalm 37:4).

92 "The steps of a good man are ordered by the Lord: and He delighteth in his way. Though he fall, he shall not be utterly cast down: for the Lord upholdeth him with His hand," (Psalm 37:23-24).

93 "But the salvation of the righteous is of the Lord: He is their strength in the time of trouble," (Psalm 37:39).

94 "For in Thee, O Lord, do I hope: Thou wilt hear, O Lord my God," (Psalm 38:15).

95 "I waited patiently for the Lord; and He inclined unto me, and heard my cry. He brought me up also out of an horrible pit, out of the miry clay, and set my feet upon a rock, and established my goings. And He hath put a new song in my mouth, even praise unto our God: many shall see it, and fear, and shall trust in the Lord," (Psalm 40:1-3).

96 "Blessed is he that considereth the poor: the Lord will deliver him in time of trouble," (Psalm 41:1).

97 "The Lord will preserve him, and keep him alive, and he shall be blessed upon the earth: and Thou wilt not deliver him unto the will of his enemies," (Psalm 41:2).

98 "The Lord will strengthen him upon the bed of languishing: Thou wilt make all his bed in his sickness," (Psalm 41:3).

99 "I said, Lord, be merciful unto me: heal my soul; for I have sinned against Thee," (Psalm 41:4).

100 "Why art thou cast down, O my soul? and why art thou disquieted in me? hope thou in God: for I shall yet praise Him for the help of His countenance," (Psalm 42:5).

101 "Why art thou cast down, O my soul? and why art thou disquieted within me? hope thou in God: for I shall yet praise Him, Who is the health of my countenance, and my God," (Psalm 42:11).

102 "God is our refuge and strength, a very present help in trouble. Therefore will not we fear, though the earth be removed, and though the mountains be carried into the midst of the sea," (Psalm 46:1-2).

103 "And call upon Me in the day of trouble: I will deliver thee, and thou shalt glorify Me," (Psalm 50:15).

104 "Evening, and morning, and at noon, will I pray, and cry aloud: and He shall hear my voice," (Psalm 55:17).

105 "Cast thy burden upon the Lord, and He shall sustain thee: He shall never suffer the righteous to be moved," (Psalm 55:22).

106 "What time I am afraid, I will trust in Thee," (Psalm 56:3).

107 "That Thy way may be known upon earth, Thy saving health among all nations," (Psalm 67:2).

108 "For Thou art my hope, O Lord God: Thou art my trust from my youth," (Psalm 71:5).

109 "But I will hope continually, and will yet praise Thee more and more," (Psalm 71:14).

110 "Therefore pride compasseth them about as a chain; violence covereth them as a garment," (Psalm 73:6).

111 "That they might set their hope in God, and not forget the works of God, but keep His commandments," (Psalm 78:7).

112 "For the Lord God is a sun and shield: the Lord will give grace and glory: no good thing will He withhold from them that walk uprightly," (Psalm 84:11).

113 "In the day of my trouble I will call upon Thee: for Thou wilt answer me. For Thou art great, and doest wondrous things: Thou art God alone. For great is Thy mercy toward me: and Thou hast delivered my soul from the lowest hell," (Psalm 86:7, 10, 13).

114 "Surely He shall deliver thee from the snare of the fowler, and from the noisome pestilence. He shall cover thee with His feathers, and under His wings shalt thou trust: His truth shall be thy shield and buckler," (Psalm 91:3-4).

115 "There shall no evil befall thee, neither shall any plague come nigh thy dwelling. For He shall give His angels charge over thee, to keep thee in all thy ways," (Psalm 91:10-11).

116 "He shall call upon me, and I will answer Him: I will be with Him in trouble; I will deliver Him, and honour Him. With long life will I satisfy Him, and shew Him my salvation," (Psalm 91:15-16).

117 "The righteous shall flourish like the palm tree: he shall grow like a cedar in Lebanon. Those that be planted in the house of the Lord shall flourish in the courts of our God. They shall still bring forth fruit in old age; they shall be fat and flourishing," (Psalm 92:12-14).

118 "He will regard the prayer of the destitute, and not despise their prayer," (Psalm 102:17).

119 "Bless the Lord, O my soul: and all that is within me, bless His holy name," (Psalm 103:1).

120 "Bless the Lord, O my soul, and forget not all His benefits," (Psalm 103:2).

121 "Who forgiveth all thine iniquities; Who healeth all thy diseases," (Psalm 103:3).

122 "Who redeemeth thy life from destruction; Who crowneth thee with lovingkindness and tender mercies," (Psalm 103:4).

123 "For He knoweth our frame; He remembereth that we are dust," (Psalm 103:14).

124 "For He satisfieth the longing soul, and filleth the hungry soul with goodness. Such as sit in darkness and in the shadow of death, being bound in affliction and iron," (Psalm 107:9-10).

125 "Then they cried unto the Lord in their trouble, and He saved them out of their distresses. He brought them out of darkness and the shadow of death, and brake their bands in sunder," (Psalm 107:13-14).

126 "He sent His word, and healed them, and delivered them from their destructions," (Psalm 107:20).

127 "He maketh the storm a calm, so that the waves thereof are still. Then are they glad because they be quiet; so He bringeth them unto their desired haven," (Psalm 107:29-30).

128 "The works of the Lord are great, sought out of all them that have pleasure therein. His work is honourable and glorious: and His righteousness endureth for ever. He hath made His wonderful works to be remembered: the Lord is gracious and full of compassion," (Psalm 111:2-4).

129 "Return unto thy rest, O my soul; for the Lord hath dealt bountifully with thee. For Thou hast delivered my soul from death, mine eyes from tears, and my feet from falling," (Psalm 116:7-8).

130 "The Lord is on my side; I will not fear," (Psalm 118:6).

131 "I shall not die, but live, and declare the works of the Lord," (Psalm 118:17).

132 "Blessed are they that keep His testimonies, and that seek Him with the whole heart," (Psalm 119:2).

133 "This is my comfort in my affliction: for Thy word hath quickened me," (Psalm 119:50).

134 "It is good for me that I have been afflicted; that I might learn Thy statutes," (Psalm 119:71).

135 "Thou art my hiding place and my shield: I hope in Thy word," (Psalm 119:114).

136 "Uphold me according unto Thy word, that I may live: and let me not be ashamed of my hope," (Psalm 119:116).

137 "I will lift up mine eyes unto the hills, from whence cometh my help. My help cometh from the Lord, which made heaven and earth. He will not suffer thy foot to be moved: He that keepeth thee will not slumber," (Psalm 121:1-3).

138 "The Lord is thy keeper: the Lord is thy shade upon thy right hand. The sun shall not smite thee by day, nor the moon by night. The Lord shall preserve thee from all evil: He shall preserve thy soul. The Lord shall preserve thy going out and thy coming in from this time forth, and even for evermore," (Psalm 121:5-8).

139 "Our soul is escaped as a bird out of the snare of the fowlers: the snare is broken, and we are escaped. Our help is in the name of the Lord, Who made heaven and earth," (Psalm 124:7-8).

140 "They that trust in the Lord shall be as mount Zion, which cannot be removed, but abideth for ever," (Psalm 125:1).

141 "The Lord hath done great things for us; whereof we are glad," (Psalm 126:3).

142 "They that sow in tears shall reap in joy," (Psalm 126:5).

143 "I wait for the Lord, my soul doth wait, and in His word do I hope," (Psalm 130:5).

144 "In the day when I cried Thou answeredst me, and strengthenedst me with strength in my soul. Though I walk in the midst of trouble, Thou wilt revive me: Thou shalt stretch forth thine hand against the wrath of mine enemies, and Thy right hand shall save me. The Lord will perfect that which concerneth me: Thy mercy, O Lord, endureth for ever: forsake not the works of Thine own hands," (Psalm 138:3, 7-8).

145 "If I ascend up into heaven, Thou art there: if I make my bed in hell, behold, Thou art there. Even there shall Thy hand lead me, and Thy right hand shall hold me," (Psalm 139:8, 10).

146 "The Lord upholdeth all that fall, and raiseth up all those that be bowed down," (Psalm 145:14).

147 "The Lord is nigh unto all them that call upon Him, to all that call upon Him in truth. He will fulfil the desire of them that fear Him: He also will hear their cry, and will save them," (Psalm 145:18-19).

148 "Happy is he that hath the God of Jacob for his help, whose hope is in the Lord his God," (Psalm 146:5).

149 "The Lord openeth the eyes of the blind: the Lord raiseth them that are bowed down: the Lord loveth the righteous," (Psalm 146:8).

150 "He healeth the broken in heart, and bindeth up their wounds," (Psalm 147:3).

151 "The Lord taketh pleasure in them that fear Him, in those that hope in His mercy," (Psalm 147:11).

152 "Trust in the Lord with all thine heart; and lean not unto thine own understanding," (Proverbs 3:5).

153 "Be not wise in thine own eyes: fear the Lord, and depart from evil. It shall be health to thy navel, and marrow to thy bones," (Proverbs 3:7-8).

154 "Then shalt thou walk in thy way safely, and thy foot shall not stumble. When thou liest down, thou shalt not be afraid: yea, thou shalt lie down, and thy sleep shall be sweet," (Proverbs 3:23-24).

155 "My son, attend to My words; incline thine ear unto My sayings. Let them not depart from thine eyes; keep them in the midst of thine heart. For they are life unto those that find them, and health to all their flesh," (Proverbs 4:20-22).

156 "Keep thy heart with all diligence; for out of it are the issues of life," (Proverbs 4:23).

157 "I love them that love Me; and those that seek Me early shall find Me," (Proverbs 8:17).

158 "There is that speaketh like the piercings of a sword: but the tongue of the wise is health," (Proverbs 12:18).

159 "A wicked messenger falleth into mischief: but a faithful ambassador is health," (Proverbs 13:17).

160 "Pleasant words are as an honeycomb, sweet to the soul, and health to the bones," (Proverbs 16:24).

161 "A merry heart doeth good like a medicine," (Proverbs 17:22).

162 "The name of the Lord is a strong tower: the righteous runneth into it, and is safe," (Proverbs 18:10).

163 "A time to kill, and a time to heal; a time to break down, and a time to build up," (Ecclesiastes 3:3).

164 "Make the heart of this people fat, and make their ears heavy, and shut their eyes; lest they see with their eyes, and hear with their ears, and understand with their heart, and convert, and be healed," (Isaiah 6:10).

165 "And it shall come to pass in that day, that his burden shall be taken away from off thy shoulder, and his yoke from off thy neck, and the yoke shall be destroyed because of the anointing," (Isaiah 10:27).

166 "And it shall come to pass in the day that the Lord shall give thee rest from thy sorrow, and from thy fear, and from the hard bondage wherein thou wast made to serve," (Isaiah 14:3).

167 "And the Lord shall smite Egypt: He shall smite and heal it: and they shall return even to the Lord, and He shall be intreated of them, and shall heal them," (Isaiah 19:22).

168 "O Lord, Thou art my God; I will exalt Thee, I will praise Thy name; for Thou hast done wonderful things; Thy counsels of old are faithfulness and truth. For Thou hast been a strength to the poor, a strength to the needy in his distress, a refuge from the storm, a shadow from the heat, when the blast of the terrible ones is as a storm against the wall," (Isaiah 25:1, 4).

169 "Thou wilt keep him in perfect peace, whose mind is stayed on Thee: because he trusteth in Thee," (Isaiah 26:3).

170 "And the work of righteousness shall be peace; and the effect of righteousness quietness and assurance for ever. And My people shall dwell in a peaceable habitation, and in sure dwellings, and in quiet resting places," (Isaiah 32:17-18).

171 "Then the eyes of the blind shall be opened, and the ears of the deaf shall be unstopped. Then shall the lame man leap as an hart, and the tongue of the dumb sing: for in the wilderness shall waters break out, and streams in the desert. And the parched ground shall become a pool, and the thirsty land springs of water: in the habitation of dragons, where each lay, shall be grass with reeds and rushes," (Isaiah 35:5-7).

172 "The writing of Hezekiah king of Judah, when he had been sick, and was recovered of his sickness," (Isaiah 38:9).

173 "Every valley shall be exalted, and every mountain and hill shall be made low: and the crooked shall be made straight, and the rough places plain: And the glory of the Lord shall be revealed, and all flesh shall see it together: for the mouth of the Lord hath spoken it," (Isaiah 40:4-5).

174 "He shall feed His flock like a shepherd: He shall gather the lambs with His arm, and carry them in His bosom, and shall gently lead those that are with young," (Isaiah 40:11).

175 "Hast thou not known? hast thou not heard, that the everlasting God, the Lord, the Creator of the ends of the earth, fainteth not, neither is weary? there is no searching of His understanding. He giveth power to the faint; and to them that have no might He increaseth strength," (Isaiah 40:28-29).

176 "Fear thou not; for I am with thee: be not dismayed; for I am thy God: I will strengthen thee; yea, I will help thee; yea, I will uphold thee with the right hand of My righteousness," (Isaiah 41:10).

177 "When the poor and needy seek water, and there is none, and their tongue faileth for thirst, I the Lord will hear them, I the God of Israel will not forsake them. I will open rivers in high places, and fountains in the midst of the valleys: I will make the wilderness a pool of water, and the dry land springs of water," (Isaiah 41:17-18).

178 "When thou passest through the waters, I will be with thee; and through the rivers, they shall not overflow thee: when thou walkest through the fire, thou shalt not be burned; neither shall the flame kindle upon thee," (Isaiah 43:2).

179 "Behold, I will do a new thing; now it shall spring forth; shall ye not know it? I will even make a way in the wilderness, and rivers in the desert," (Isaiah 43:19).

180 "For I will pour water upon him that is thirsty, and floods upon the dry ground: I will pour My spirit upon thy seed, and My blessing upon thine offspring: And they shall spring up as among the grass, as willows by the water courses," (Isaiah 44:3-4).

181 "Thus saith the Lord, the Holy One of Israel, and His Maker, Ask me of things to come concerning my sons, and concerning the work of my hands command ye me," (Isaiah 45:11).

182 "Sing, O heavens; and be joyful, O earth; and break forth into singing, O mountains: for the Lord hath comforted His people, and will have mercy upon His afflicted," (Isaiah 49:13).

183 "Can a woman forget her sucking child, that she should not have compassion on the son of her womb? yea, they may forget, yet will I not forget thee. Behold, I have graven thee upon the palms of My hands; thy walls are continually before Me," (Isaiah 49:15-16).

184 "The Lord God hath given me the tongue of the learned, that I should know how to speak a word in season to him that is weary: He wakeneth morning by morning, He wakeneth mine ear to hear as the learned," (Isaiah 50:4).

185 "Surely He hath borne our griefs, and carried our sorrows: yet we did esteem Him stricken, smitten of God, and afflicted," (Isaiah 53:4).

186 "But He was wounded for our transgressions, He was bruised for our iniquities: the chastisement of our peace was upon Him; and with His stripes we are healed," (Isaiah 53:5).

187 "For the mountains shall depart, and the hills be removed; but My kindness shall not depart from thee, neither shall the covenant of My peace be removed, saith the Lord that hath mercy on thee," (Isaiah 54:10).

188 "No weapon that is formed against thee shall prosper," (Isaiah 54:17).

189 "Seek ye the Lord while He may be found, call ye upon Him while He is near," (Isaiah 55:6).

190 "So shall My word be that goeth forth out of My mouth," (Isaiah 55:11).

191 "I have seen his ways, and will heal him: I will lead him also, and restore comforts unto him and to his mourners," (Isaiah 57:18).

192 "I create the fruit of the lips; Peace, peace to him that is far off, and to him that is near, saith the

Lord; and I will heal him," (Isaiah 57:19).

193 "Is not this the fast that I have chosen? to loose the bands of wickedness, to undo the heavy burdens, and to let the oppressed go free, and that ye break every yoke?" (Isaiah 58:6).

194 "Then shall thy light break forth as the morning, and thine health shall spring forth speedily," (Isaiah 58:8).

195 "Behold, the Lord's hand is not shortened, that it cannot save; neither His ear heavy, that it cannot hear," (Isaiah 59:1).

196 "Arise, shine; for thy light is come, and the glory of the Lord is risen upon thee. For, behold, the darkness shall cover the earth, and gross darkness the people: but the Lord shall arise upon thee, and his glory shall be seen upon thee. And the Gentiles shall come to thy light, and kings to the brightness of thy rising," (Isaiah 60:1-3).

197 "The Spirit of the Lord God is upon me; because the Lord hath anointed me to preach good tidings unto the meek: He hath sent me to bind up the brokenhearted, to proclaim liberty to the captives, and the opening of the prison to them that are bound," (Isaiah 61:1).

198 "To appoint unto them that mourn in Zion, to give unto them beauty for ashes, the oil of joy for mourning, the garment of praise for the spirit of heaviness; that they might be called trees of righteousness, the planting of the Lord, that He might be glorified," (Isaiah 61:3).

199 "And it shall come to pass, that before they call, I will answer; and while they are yet speaking, I will hear," (Isaiah 65:24).

200 "I will hasten my word to perform it," (Jeremiah 1:12).

201 "Return, ye backsliding children, and I will heal your backslidings. Behold, we come unto Thee; for Thou art the Lord our God," (Jeremiah 3:22).

202 "Heal me, O Lord, and I shall be healed; save me, and I shall be saved: for Thou art my praise," (Jeremiah 17:14).

203 "Blessed is the man that trusteth in the Lord, and whose hope the Lord is," (Jeremiah 17:7).

204 "For I know the thoughts that I think toward you, saith the Lord, thoughts of peace, and not of evil, to give you an expected end. Then shall ye call upon Me, and ye shall go and pray unto Me, and I will hearken unto you. And ye shall seek Me, and find Me, when ye shall search for Me with all your heart," (Jeremiah 29:11-13).

205 "For I will restore health unto thee, and I will heal thee of thy wounds, saith the Lord; because they called thee an Outcast, saying, This is Zion, whom no man seeketh after," (Jeremiah 30:17).

206 "Ah Lord God! behold, Thou hast made the heaven and the earth by Thy great power and stretched out arm, and there is nothing too hard for Thee," (Jeremiah 32:17).

207 "Behold, I am the Lord, the God of all flesh: is there any thing too hard for Me?" (Jeremiah 32:27).

208 "Call unto Me, and I will answer thee, and shew thee great and mighty things, which thou knowest not," (Jeremiah 33:3).

209 "Behold, I will bring it health and cure, and I will cure them, and will reveal unto them the abundance of peace and truth," (Jeremiah 33:6).

210 "Behold, the days come, saith the Lord, that I will perform that good thing which I have promised," (Jeremiah 33:14).

211 "For I will surely deliver thee, and thou shalt not fall by the sword, but thy life shall be for a prey unto thee: because thou hast put thy trust in Me, saith the Lord," (Jeremiah 39:18).

212 "The Lord is my portion, saith my soul; therefore will I hope in Him," (Lamentations 3:24).

213 "I will seek that which was lost, and bring again that which was driven away, and will bind up

that which was broken, and will strengthen that which was sick," (Ezekiel 34:16).

214 "For, behold, I am for you," (Ezekiel 36:9).

215 "And it shall come to pass, that every thing that liveth, which moveth, whithersoever the rivers shall come, shall live: and there shall be a very great multitude of fish, because these waters shall come thither: for they shall be healed; and every thing shall live whither the river cometh," (Ezekiel 47:9).

216 "He delivereth and rescueth, and He worketh signs and wonders in heaven and in earth, Who hath delivered Daniel from the power of the lions," (Daniel 6:27).

217 "Come, and let us return unto the Lord: for He hath torn, and He will heal us; He hath smitten, and He will bind us up," (Hosea 6:1).

218 "I will heal their backsliding, I will love them freely: for Mine anger is turned away from him," (Hosea 14:4).

219 "And I will restore to you the years that the locust hath eaten," (Joel 2:25).

220 "Seek the Lord, and ye shall live," (Amos 5:6).

221 "But unto you that fear My name shall the Sun of righteousness arise with healing in His wings; and ye shall go forth, and grow up as calves of the stall," (Malachi 4:2).

222 "And Jesus went about all Galilee, teaching in their synagogues, and preaching the gospel of the kingdom, and healing all manner of sickness and all manner of disease among the people," (Matthew 4:23).

223 "And His fame went throughout all Syria: and they brought unto Him all sick people that were taken with divers diseases and torments, and those which were possessed with devils, and those which were lunatick, and those that had the palsy; and He healed them," (Matthew 4:24).

224 "But seek ye first the kingdom of God, and His righteousness; and all these things shall be added unto you," (Matthew 6:33).

225 "Ask, and it shall be given you; seek, and ye shall find; knock, and it shall be opened unto you," (Matthew 7:7).

226 "For every one that asketh receiveth; and he that seeketh findeth; and to him that knocketh it shall be opened," (Matthew 7:8).

227 "Or what man is there of you, whom if his son ask bread, will he give him a stone? Or if he ask a fish, will he give him a serpent? If ye then, being evil, know how to give good gifts unto your children, how much more shall your Father which is in heaven give good things to them that ask Him?" (Matthew 7:9-11).

228 "And Jesus put forth His hand, and touched him, saying, I will; be thou clean. And immediately his leprosy was cleansed," (Matthew 8:3).

229 "And Jesus saith unto him, I will come and heal him," (Matthew 8:7).

230 "The centurion answered and said, Lord, I am not worthy that Thou shouldest come under my roof: but speak the word only, and my servant shall be healed," (Matthew 8:8).

231 "And Jesus said unto the centurion, Go thy way; and as thou hast believed, so be it done unto thee. And his servant was healed in the selfsame hour," (Matthew 8:13).

232 "And He touched her hand, and the fever left her: and she arose, and ministered unto them," (Matthew 8:15).

233 "When the even was come, they brought unto Him many that were possessed with devils: and He cast out the spirits with His word, and healed all that were sick," (Matthew 8:16).

234 "That it might be fulfilled which was spoken by Esaias the prophet, saying, Himself took our infirmities, and bare our sicknesses," (Matthew 8:17).

235 "And, behold, they brought to Him a man sick of the palsy, lying on a bed: and Jesus seeing their faith said unto the sick of the palsy; Son, be of good cheer; thy sins be forgiven thee," (Matthew 9:2).

236 "For whether is easier, to say, Thy sins be forgiven thee; or to say, Arise, and walk? But that ye may know that the Son of man hath power on earth to forgive sins, (then saith He to the sick of the palsy,) Arise, take up thy bed, and go unto thine house," (Matthew 9:5-6).

237 "But Jesus turned him about, and when He saw her, He said, Daughter, be of good comfort; thy faith hath made thee whole. And the woman was made whole from that hour," (Matthew 9:22).

238 "Then touched He their eyes, saying, According to your faith be it unto you," (Matthew 9:29).

239 "And Jesus went about all the cities and villages, teaching in their synagogues, and preaching the gospel of the kingdom, and healing every sickness and every disease among the people," (Matthew 9:35).

240 "And when He had called unto Him His twelve disciples, He gave them power against unclean spirits, to cast them out, and to heal all manner of sickness and all manner of disease," (Matthew 10:1).

241 "Heal the sick, cleanse the lepers, raise the dead, cast out devils: freely ye have received,

freely give," (Matthew 10:8).

242 "The blind receive their sight, and the lame walk, the lepers are cleansed, and the deaf hear, the dead are raised up, and the poor have the gospel preached to them," (Matthew 11:5).

243 "Then saith He to the man, Stretch forth thine hand. And he stretched it forth; and it was restored whole, like as the other," (Matthew 12:13).

244 "But when Jesus knew it, He withdrew Himself from thence: and great multitudes followed Him, and He healed them all," (Matthew 12:15).

245 "Then was brought unto Him one possessed with a devil, blind, and dumb: and He healed him, insomuch that the blind and dumb both spake and saw," (Matthew 12:22).

246 "For this people's heart is waxed gross, and their ears are dull of hearing, and their eyes they have closed; lest at any time they should see with their eyes, and hear with their ears, and should understand with their heart, and should be converted, and I should heal them," (Matthew 13:15).

247 "And Jesus went forth, and saw a great multitude, and was moved with compassion toward them, and He healed their sick," (Matthew 14:14).

248 "And when the men of that place had knowledge of Him, they sent out into all that country round about, and brought unto Him all that were diseased: And besought Him that they might only touch the hem of His garment; and as many as touched were made perfectly whole," (Matthew 14:35-36).

249 "Then Jesus answered and said unto her, O woman, great is thy faith: be it unto thee even as thou wilt. And her daughter was made whole from that very hour," (Matthew 15:28).

250 "And great multitudes came unto Him, having with them those that were lame, blind, dumb, maimed, and many others, and cast them down at Jesus' feet; and He healed them: Insomuch that the multitude wondered, when they saw the dumb to speak, the maimed to be whole, the lame to walk, and the blind to see: and they glorified the God of Israel," (Matthew 15:30-31).

251 "And Jesus came and touched them, and said, Arise, and be not afraid," (Matthew 17:7).

252 "And Jesus said unto them, Because of your unbelief: for verily I say unto you, If ye have faith as a grain of mustard seed, ye shall say unto this mountain, Remove hence to yonder place; and it shall remove; and nothing shall be impossible unto you," (Matthew 17:20).

253 "Verily I say unto you, Whatsoever ye shall bind on earth shall be bound in heaven: and whatsoever ye shall loose on earth shall be loosed in heaven," (Matthew 18:18).

254 "Again I say unto you, That if two of you shall agree on earth as touching any thing that they shall ask, it shall be done for them of My Father which is in heaven," (Matthew 18:19).

255 "And a great multitudes followed Him; and He healed them there," (Matthew 19:2).

256 "But Jesus beheld them, and said unto them, With men this is impossible: but with God all things are possible," (Matthew 19:26).

257 "So Jesus had compassion on them, and touched their eyes: and immediately their eyes received sight, and they followed Him," (Matthew 20:34).

258 "And the blind and the lame came to Him in the temple; and He healed them," (Matthew 21:14).

259 "Jesus answered and said unto them, Verily I say unto you, If ye have faith, and doubt not, ye shall not only do this which is done to the fig tree, but also if ye shall say unto this mountain, Be thou removed, and be thou cast into the sea; it shall be done," (Matthew 21:21).

260 "And at even, when the sun did set, they brought unto Him all that were diseased, and them that were possessed with devils. And all the city was gathered together at the door. And He healed many that were sick of divers diseases, and cast out many devils; and suffered not the devils to speak, because they knew Him," (Mark 1:32-34).

261 "And Jesus, moved with compassion, put forth His hand, and touched him, and saith unto him, I will; be thou clean," (Mark 1:41).

262 "When Jesus saw their faith, He said unto the sick of the palsy, Son, thy sins be forgiven thee," (Mark 2:5).

263 "I say unto thee, Arise, and take up thy bed, and go thy way into thine house," (Mark 2:11).

264 "And when He had looked round about on them with anger, being grieved for the hardness of their hearts, He saith unto the man, Stretch forth thine hand. And he stretched it out: and his hand was restored whole as the other," (Mark 3:5).

265 "For He had healed many; insomuch that they pressed upon Him for to touch Him, as many as had plagues," (Mark 3:10).

266 "And He ordained twelve, that they should be with Him, and that He might send them forth to preach, And to have power to heal sicknesses, and to cast out devils," (Mark 3:14-15).

267 "For she said, If I may touch but His clothes, I shall be whole. And straightway the fountain of her blood was dried up; and she felt in her body that she was healed of that plague. And Jesus, immediately knowing in Himself that virtue had gone out of Him, turned Him about in the press, and said, Who touched My clothes? And He said unto her,

Daughter, thy faith hath made thee whole; go in peace, and be whole of thy plague," (Mark 5:28-30, 34).

268 "And He took the damsel by the hand, and said unto her, Talitha cumi; which is, being interpreted, Damsel, I say unto thee, arise," (Mark 5:41).

269 "And He could there do no mighty work, save that He laid His hands upon a few sick folk, and healed them," (Mark 6:5).

270 "And He called unto Him the twelve, and began to send them forth by two and two; and gave them power over unclean spirits; And they went out, and preached that men should repent. And they cast out many devils, and anointed with oil many that were sick, and healed them," (Mark 6:7, 12-13).

271 "And whithersoever He entered, into villages, or cities, or country, they laid the sick in the streets, and besought Him that they might touch if it were but the border of His garment: and as many as touched Him were made whole," (Mark 6:56).

272 "Jesus said unto him, If thou canst believe, all things are possible to him that believeth," (Mark 9:23).

273 "And Jesus looking upon them saith, With men it is impossible, but not with God: for with God all things are possible," (Mark 10:27).

274 "And Jesus said unto him, Go thy way; thy faith hath made thee whole. And immediately he received his sight, and followed Jesus in the way," (Mark 10:52).

275 "And Jesus answering saith unto them, Have faith in God," (Mark 11:22).

276 "For verily I say unto you, That whosoever shall say unto this mountain, Be thou removed, and be thou cast into the sea; and shall not doubt in his heart, but shall believe that those things which he saith shall come to pass; he shall have whatsoever he saith," (Mark 11:23).

277 "Therefore I say unto you, What things soever ye desire, when ye pray, believe that ye receive them, and ye shall have them," (Mark 11:24).

278 "And these signs shall follow them that believe; In my name shall they cast out devils; they shall speak with new tongues; They shall take up serpents; and if they drink any deadly thing, it shall not hurt them; they shall lay hands on the sick, and they shall recover," (Mark 16:17-18).

279 "The Spirit of the Lord is upon me, because He hath anointed me to preach the gospel to the poor; He hath sent me to heal the brokenhearted, to preach deliverance to the captives, and recovering of sight to the blind, to set at liberty them that are bruised," (Luke 4:18).

280 "Now when the sun was setting, all they that had any sick with divers diseases brought them unto Him; and He laid His hands on every one of them, and healed them," (Luke 4:40).

281 "And He put forth His hand, and touched him, saying, I will: be thou clean. And immediately the leprosy departed from him," (Luke 5:13).

282 "But so much the more went there a fame abroad of Him: and great multitudes came together to hear, and to be healed by Him of their infirmities," (Luke 5:15).

283 "And it came to pass on a certain day, as He was teaching, that there were Pharisees and doctors of the law sitting by, which were come out of every town of Galilee, and Judaea, and Jerusalem: and the power of the Lord was present to heal them," (Luke 5:17).

284 "But that ye may know that the Son of man hath power upon earth to forgive sins, (He said unto the sick of the palsy,) I say unto thee, Arise, and take up thy couch, and go into thine house," (Luke 5:24).

285 "And looking round about upon them all, He said unto the man, Stretch forth thy hand. And he did so: and his hand was restored whole as the other," (Luke 6:10).

286 "And they that were vexed with unclean spirits: and they were healed," (Luke 6:18).

287 "And the whole multitude sought to touch Him: for there went virtue out of Him, and healed them all," (Luke 6:19).

288 "For I also am a man set under authority, having under me soldiers, and I say unto one, Go, and he goeth; and to another, Come, and he cometh; and to my servant, Do this, and he doeth it. When Jesus heard these things, He marvelled at him, and turned him about, and said unto the people that followed Him, I say unto you, I have not found so great faith, no, not in Israel. And they that were sent, returning to the house, found the servant whole that had been sick," (Luke 7:8-10).

289 "Now when He came nigh to the gate of the city, behold, there was a dead man carried out, the only son of his mother, and she was a widow: and much people of the city was with her. And when the Lord saw her, He had compassion on her, and said unto her, Weep not. And He came and touched the bier: and they that bare Him stood still. And He said, Young man, I say unto thee, Arise. And he that was dead sat up, and began to speak. And He delivered him to his mother," (Luke 7:12-15).

290 "And in that same hour He cured many of their infirmities and plagues, and of evil spirits; and unto many that were blind He gave sight," (Luke 7:21).

291 "And He said to the woman, Thy faith hath saved thee; go in peace," (Luke 7:50).

292 "And certain women, which had been healed of evil spirits and infirmities, Mary called Magdalene, out of whom went seven devils," (Luke 8:2).

293 "They also which saw it told them by what means he that was possessed of the devils was healed," (Luke 8:36).

294 "Came behind Him, and touched the border of His garment: and immediately her issue of blood stanched. And Jesus said, Who touched Me? When all denied, Peter and they that were with Him said, Master, the multitude throng Thee and press Thee, and sayest Thou, Who touched Me? And Jesus said, Somebody hath touched Me: for I perceive that virtue is gone out of Me. And when the woman saw that she was not hid, she came trembling, and falling down before Him, she declared unto Him before all the people for what cause she had touched Him, and how she was healed immediately. And He said unto her, Daughter, be of good comfort: thy faith hath made thee whole; go in peace," (Luke 8:44-48).

295 "But when Jesus heard it, He answered him, saying, Fear not: believe only, and she shall be made whole," (Luke 8:50).

296 "And He put them all out, and took her by the hand, and called, saying, Maid, arise," (Luke 8:54).

297 "Then He called His twelve disciples together, and gave them power and authority over all devils, and to cure diseases. And He sent them to preach the kingdom of God, and to heal the sick," (Luke 9:1-2).

298 "And they departed, and went through the towns, preaching the gospel, and healing every where," (Luke 9:6).

299 "And the people, when they knew it, followed Him: and He received them, and spake unto them of the kingdom of God, and healed them that had need of healing," (Luke 9:11).

300 "And as he was yet a coming, the devil threw him down, and tare him. And Jesus rebuked the unclean spirit, and healed the child, and delivered him again to his father," (Luke 9:42).

301 "And heal the sick that are therein, and say unto them, The kingdom of God is come nigh unto you," (Luke 10:9).

302 "Behold, I give unto you power to tread on serpents and scorpions, and over all the power of the enemy: and nothing shall by any means hurt you," (Luke 10:19).

303 "And I say unto you, Ask, and it shall be given you; seek, and ye shall find; knock, and it shall be opened unto you. For every one that asketh receiveth; and he that seeketh findeth; and to him that knocketh it shall be opened. If a son shall ask bread of any of you that is a father, will he give him a stone? or if he ask a fish, will he for a fish give him a serpent? Or if he shall ask an egg, will he offer him a scorpion? If ye then, being evil, know how to give good gifts unto your children: how much more shall your heavenly Father give the Holy Spirit to them that ask Him?" (Luke 11:9-13).

304 "And when Jesus saw her, He called her to Him, and said unto her, Woman, thou art loosed from thine infirmity," (Luke 13:12).

305 "And they held their peace. And He took him, and healed him, and let him go," (Luke 14:4).

306 "And the Lord said, If ye had faith as a grain of mustard seed, ye might say unto this sycamine tree, Be thou plucked up by the root, and be thou planted in the sea; and it should obey you," (Luke 17:6).

307 "And one of them, when he saw that he was healed, turned back, and with a loud voice glorified God," (Luke 17:15).

308 "And He said unto him, Arise, go thy way: thy faith hath made thee whole," (Luke 17:19).

309 "And He said, The things which are impossible with men are possible with God," (Luke 18:27).

310 "And Jesus said unto Him, Receive thy sight: thy faith hath saved thee," (Luke 18:42).

311 "And Jesus answered and said, Suffer ye thus far. And He touched his ear, and healed him," (Luke 22:51).

312 "Now when He was in Jerusalem at the passover, in the feast day, many believed in His name, when they saw the miracles which He did," (John 2:23).

313 "In these lay a great multitude of impotent folk, of blind, halt, withered, waiting for the moving of the water. For an angel went down at a certain season into the pool, and troubled the water: whosoever then first after the troubling of the water stepped in was made whole of whatsoever disease he had," (John 5:3-4).

314 "And a certain man was there, which had an infirmity thirty and eight years. When Jesus saw him lie, and knew that he had been now a long time in that case, He saith unto him, Wilt thou be made whole? The impotent man answered him, Sir, I have no man, when the water is troubled, to put me into the pool: but while I am coming, another steppeth down before me. Jesus saith unto him, Rise, take up thy bed, and walk. And immediately the man was made whole, and took up his bed, and walked: and on the same day was the sabbath, He answered them, He that made me whole, the same said unto me, Take up thy bed, and walk," (John 5:5-9, 11).

315 "And he that was healed wist not who it was: for Jesus had conveyed Himself away, a multitude being in that place. Afterward Jesus findeth him in the temple, and said unto him, Behold, thou art made whole: sin no more, lest a worse thing come unto thee. The man departed, and told the Jews that it was Jesus, which had made him whole," (John 5:13-15).

316 "And a great multitude followed Him, because they saw His miracles which He did on them that were diseased," (John 6:2).

317 "The thief cometh not, but for to steal, and to kill, and to destroy: I am come that they might have life, and that they might have it more abundantly," (John 10:10).

318 "When Jesus heard that, He said, This sickness is not unto death, but for the glory of God, that the Son of God might be glorified thereby," (John 11:4).

319 "He hath blinded their eyes, and hardened their heart; that they should not see with their eyes, nor understand with their heart, and be converted, and I should heal them," (John 12:40).

320 "And whatsoever ye shall ask in My name, that will I do, that the Father may be glorified in the Son. If ye shall ask any thing in My name, I will do it," (John 14:13-14).

321 "If ye abide in Me, and My words abide in you, ye shall ask what ye will, and it shall be done unto you," (John 15:7).

322 "And in that day ye shall ask Me nothing. Verily, verily, I say unto you, Whatsoever ye shall ask the Father in My name, He will give it you. Hitherto have ye asked nothing in My name: ask, and ye shall receive, that your joy may be full," (John 16:23-24).

323 "But these are written, that ye might believe that Jesus is the Christ, the Son of God; and that believing ye might have life through His name," (John 20:31).

324 "Therefore did my heart rejoice, and my tongue was glad; moreover also my flesh shall rest in hope," (Acts 2:26).

325 "And as the lame man which was healed held Peter and John, all the people ran together unto them in the porch that is called Solomon's, greatly wondering," (Acts 3:11).

326 "And beholding the man which was healed standing with them, they could say nothing against it. Saying, What shall we do to these men? for that indeed a notable miracle hath been done by them is manifest to all them that dwell in Jerusalem; and we cannot deny it. For the man was above forty years old, on whom this miracle of healing was shewed," (Acts 4:14, 16, 22).

327 "By stretching forth thine hand to heal; and that signs and wonders may be done by the name of thy holy child Jesus," (Acts 4:30).

328 "There came also a multitude out of the cities round about unto Jerusalem, bringing sick folks, and them which were vexed with unclean spirits: and they were healed every one," (Acts 5:16).

329 "And Stephen, full of faith and power, did great wonders and miracles among the people," (Acts 6:8).

330 "And delivered him out of all his afflictions, and gave him favour and wisdom in the sight of Pharaoh king of Egypt; and He made him governor over Egypt and all his house," (Acts 7:10).

331 "For unclean spirits, crying with loud voice, came out of many that were possessed with them: and many taken with palsies, and that were lame, were healed," (Acts 8:7).

332 "And Peter said unto him, Aeneas, Jesus Christ maketh thee whole: arise, and make thy bed. And he arose immediately," (Acts 9:34).

333 "But Peter put them all forth, and kneeled down, and prayed; and turning him to the body said, Tabitha, arise. And she opened her eyes: and when she saw Peter, she sat up," (Acts 9:40).

334 "How God anointed Jesus of Nazareth with the Holy Ghost and with power: Who went about doing good, and healing all that were oppressed of the devil; for God was with Him," (Acts 10:38).

335 "The same heard Paul speak: who stedfastly beholding him, and perceiving that he had faith to be healed," (Acts 14:9).

336 "Wherefore I pray you to take some meat: for this is for your health: for there shall not an hair fall from the head of any of you," (Acts 27:34).

337 "And it came to pass, that the father of Publius lay sick of a fever and of a bloody flux: to whom Paul entered in, and prayed, and laid his hands on him, and healed him," (Acts 28:8).

338 "So when this was done, others also, which had diseases in the island, came, and were healed," (Acts 28:9).

339 "For the heart of this people is waxed gross, and their ears are dull of hearing, and their eyes have they closed; lest they should see with their eyes, and hear with their ears, and understand with their heart, and should be converted, and I should heal them," (Acts 28:27).

340 "And being not weak in faith, he considered not his own body now dead, when he was about an hundred years old, neither yet the deadness of Sara's womb: He staggered not at the promise of God through unbelief; but was strong in faith, giving glory to God," (Romans 4:19-20).

341 "And being fully persuaded that, what He had promised, He was able also to perform," (Romans 4:21).

342 "Therefore being justified by faith, we have peace with God through our Lord Jesus Christ," (Romans 5:1).

343 "By Whom also we have access by faith into this grace wherein we stand, and rejoice in hope of the glory of God," (Romans 5:2).

344 "But if the Spirit of him that raised up Jesus from the dead dwell in you," (Romans 8:11).

345 "But if we hope for that we see not, then do we with patience wait for it," (Romans 8:25).

346 "Likewise the Spirit also helpeth our infirmities: for we know not what we should pray for as we ought: but the Spirit itself maketh intercession for us with groanings which cannot be uttered," (Romans 8:26).

347 "Nay, in all these things we are more than conquerors through Him that loved us. For I am persuaded, that neither death, nor life, nor angels, nor principalities, nor powers, nor things present, nor things to come, Nor height, nor depth, nor any other creature, shall be able to separate us from the love of God, which is in Christ Jesus our Lord," (Romans 8:37-39).

348 "But what saith it? The word is nigh thee, even in thy mouth, and in thy heart: that is, the word of faith, which we preach," (Romans 10:8).

349 "So then faith cometh by hearing, and hearing by the word of God," (Romans 10:17).

350 "For whatsoever things were written aforetime were written for our learning, that we through patience and comfort of the scriptures might have hope," (Romans 15:4).

351 "Now the God of hope fill you with all joy and peace in believing, that ye may abound in hope, through the power of the Holy Ghost," (Romans 15:13).

352 "That your faith should not stand in the wisdom of men, but in the power of God," (1 Corinthians 2:5).

353 "To another faith by the same Spirit; to another the gifts of healing by the same Spirit," (1 Corinthians 12:9).

354 "To another the working of miracles; to another prophecy; to another discerning of spirits; to another divers kinds of tongues; to another the interpretation of tongues," (1 Corinthians 12:10).

355 "And God hath set some in the church, first apostles, secondarily prophets, thirdly teachers, after that miracles, then gifts of healings, helps, governments, diversities of tongues," (1 Corinthians 12:28).

356 "Watch ye, stand fast in the faith, quit you like men, be strong," (1 Corinthians 16:13).

357 "And our hope of you is stedfast, knowing, that as ye are partakers of the sufferings, so shall ye be also of the consolation," (2 Corinthians 1:7).

358 "Now thanks be unto God, which always causeth us to triumph in Christ, and maketh manifest the savour of His knowledge by us in every place," (2 Corinthians 2:14).

359 "For our light affliction, which is but for a moment, worketh for us a far more exceeding and eternal weight of glory," (2 Corinthians 4:17).

360 "For we walk by faith, not by sight," (2 Corinthians 5:7).

361 "For the weapons of our warfare are not carnal, but mighty through God to the pulling down of strong holds," (2 Corinthians 10:4).

362 "I am crucified with Christ: nevertheless I live; yet not I, but Christ liveth in me: and the life which I now live in the flesh I live by the faith of the Son of God, Who loved me, and gave Himself for me," (Galatians 2:20).

363 "Christ hath redeemed us from the curse of the law," (Galatians 3:13).

364 "For ye are all the children of God by faith in Christ Jesus," (Galatians 3:26).

365 "And what is the exceeding greatness of His power to us-ward who believe, according to the working of His mighty power," (Ephesians 1:19).

366 "In Whom we have boldness and access with confidence by the faith of Him," (Ephesians 3:12).

367 "Wherefore he saith, Awake thou that sleepest, and arise from the dead, and Christ shall give thee light," (Ephesians 5:14).

368 "Finally, my brethren, be strong in the Lord, and in the power of His might. Put on the whole armour of God, that ye may be able to stand against the wiles of the devil. For we wrestle not against flesh and blood, but against principalities, against powers, against the rulers of the darkness of this world, against spiritual wickedness in high places," (Ephesians 6:10-12).

369 "Above all, taking the shield of faith, wherewith ye shall be able to quench all the fiery darts of the wicked," (Ephesians 6:16).

370 "Being confident of this very thing, that He which hath begun a good work in you will perform it until the day of Jesus Christ," (Philippians 1:6).

371 "So that my bonds in Christ are manifest in all the palace, and in all other places," (Philippians 1:13).

372 "If ye continue in the faith grounded and settled, and be not moved away from the hope of the gospel, which ye have heard, and which was preached to every creature which is under heaven; whereof I Paul am made a minister," (Colossians 1:23).

373 "Rooted and built up in Him, and stablished in the faith, as ye have been taught, abounding therein with thanksgiving," (Colossians 2:7).

374 "But the Lord is faithful, Who shall stablish you, and keep you from evil," (2 Thessalonians 3:3).

375 "For God hath not given us the spirit of fear; but of power, and of love, and of a sound mind," (2 Timothy 1:7).

376 "And the Lord shall deliver me from every evil work, and will preserve me unto His heavenly kingdom: to Whom be glory for ever and ever," (2 Timothy 4:18).

377 "That the communication of thy faith may become effectual by the acknowledging of every good thing which is in you in Christ Jesus," (Philemon 1:6).

378 "Seeing then that we have a great high priest, that is passed into the heavens, Jesus the Son of God, let us hold fast our profession. For we have not an high priest which cannot be touched with the feeling of our infirmities; but was in all points tempted like as we are, yet without sin. Let us therefore come boldly unto the throne of grace," (Hebrews 4:14-16).

379 "Wherefore He is able also to save them to the uttermost that come unto God by Him, seeing

He ever liveth to make intercession for them," (Hebrews 7:25).

380 "Let us hold fast the profession of our faith without wavering; for He is faithful that promised," (Hebrews 10:23).

381 "But call to remembrance the former days, in which, after ye were illuminated, ye endured a great fight of afflictions; Cast not away therefore your confidence, which hath great recompence of reward. For ye have need of patience, that, after ye have done the will of God, ye might receive the promise," (Hebrews 10:32, 35-36).

382 "Now faith is the substance of things hoped for, the evidence of things not seen. For by it the elders obtained a good report," (Hebrews 11:1-2).

383 "But without faith it is impossible to please Him: for he that cometh to God must believe that He is, and that He is a rewarder of them that diligently seek Him," (Hebrews 11:6).

384 "Looking unto Jesus the author and finisher of our faith; Who for the joy that was set before Him endured the cross, despising the shame, and is set down at the right hand of the throne of God," (Hebrews 12:2).

385 "Let your conversation be without covetousness; and be content with such things as ye have: for He hath said, I will never leave thee, nor forsake thee," (Hebrews 13:5).

386 "Jesus Christ the same yesterday, and to day, and for ever," (Hebrews 13:8).

387 "But let him ask in faith, nothing wavering. For he that wavereth is like a wave of the sea driven with the wind and tossed," (James 1:6).

388 "Every good gift and every perfect gift is from above, and cometh down from the Father of lights, with whom is no variableness, neither shadow of turning," (James 1:17).

389 "Is any among you afflicted? let him pray. Is any merry? let him sing psalms," (James 5:13).

390 "Is any sick among you? let him call for the elders of the church; and let them pray over him, anointing him with oil in the name of the Lord," (James 5:14).

391 "And the prayer of faith shall save the sick, and the Lord shall raise him up; and if he have committed sins, they shall be forgiven him," (James 5:15).

392 "Confess your faults one to another, and pray one for another, that ye may be healed. The effectual fervent prayer of a righteous man availeth much," (James 5:16).

393 "Blessed be the God and Father of our Lord Jesus Christ, which according to His abundant mercy hath begotten us again unto a lively hope by the resurrection of Jesus Christ from the dead," (1 Peter 1:3).

394 "Wherein ye greatly rejoice, though now for a season, if need be, ye are in heaviness through manifold temptations: That the trial of your faith, being much more precious than of gold that perisheth, though it be tried with fire, might be found unto praise and honour and glory at the appearing of Jesus Christ," (1 Peter 1:6-7).

395 "Who by Him do believe in God, that raised Him up from the dead, and gave Him glory; that your faith and hope might be in God," (1 Peter 1:21).

396 "Who His own self bare our sins in His own body on the tree, that we, being dead to sins, should live unto righteousness: by Whose stripes ye were healed," (1 Peter 2:24).

397 "Beloved, think it not strange concerning the fiery trial which is to try you, as though some strange thing happened unto you: But rejoice, inasmuch as ye are partakers of Christ's sufferings; that, when His glory shall be revealed, ye may be glad also with exceeding joy," (1 Peter 4:12-13).

398 "Casting all your care upon Him, for He careth for you," (1 Peter 5:7).

399 "But the God of all grace, Who hath called us unto His eternal glory by Christ Jesus, after that ye have suffered a while, make you perfect, stablish, strengthen, settle you," (1 Peter 5:10).

400 "And every man that hath this hope in Him purifieth himself, even as He is pure," (1 John 3:3).

401 "And whatsoever we ask, we receive of Him, because we keep His commandments, and do those things that are pleasing in His sight," (1 John 3:22).

402 "For whatsoever is born of God overcometh the world: and this is the victory that overcometh the world, even our faith," (1 John 5:4).

403 "And this is the confidence that we have in Him, that, if we ask any thing according to His will, He heareth us," (1 John 5:14).

404 "And if we know that He hear us, whatsoever we ask, we know that we have the petitions that we desired of Him," (1 John 5:15).

405 "Beloved, I wish above all things that thou mayest prosper and be in health, even as thy soul prospereth," (3 John 1:2).

406 "But ye, beloved, building up yourselves on your most holy faith, praying in the Holy Ghost," (Jude 1:20).

407 "And He shewed me a pure river of water of life, clear as crystal, proceeding out of the throne of God and of the Lamb. In the midst of the street of it, and on either side of the river, was there the tree of life, which bare twelve manner of fruits, and yielded her fruit every month: and the leaves of the tree were for the healing of the nations," (Revelation 22:1-2).

Pray This Prayer Aloud With Me Now...
"Precious Father, I love You with my whole heart. I am thankful for every good thing that has come from You. You are my Source, my Provider, my Deliverer and my Healer. That is why I serve You, trust You and approach You with boldness and great expectation of the miracle I need today.

I come to You in the powerful Name of Jesus of Nazareth, by Whose stripes I am healed. I take authority over all disease, all disorder, all pain and all sickness in my body. In the Name of Jesus, I command all pain and disease to leave my body now and forever. I am Your child, Your property, and Your temple where You abide and live as the Force of my life. I receive Your Word as Your Covenant with me for Divine health and Divine healing. I choose to believe that You are my Healer, my Deliverer, my Saviour and my King. Disease and sickness cannot reign nor rule in my body from this day forward. I declare and believe this both publicly and privately under the authority of the Name of Jesus. It is done. Amen."

Will you pray about becoming my monthly partner? Your Seed each month will unleash a new anointing for the Wisdom of God in your life.

Mike

DECISION

Will You Accept Jesus As Your Personal Savior Today?

The Bible says, "That if thou shalt confess with thy mouth the Lord Jesus, and shalt believe in thine heart that God hath raised Him from the dead, thou shalt be saved," (Romans 10:9).

Pray this prayer from your heart today!

"Dear Jesus, I believe that You died for me and rose again on the third day. I confess I am a sinner...I need Your love and forgiveness...Come into my heart. Forgive my sins. I receive Your eternal life. Confirm Your love by giving me peace, joy and supernatural love for others. Amen."

DR. MIKE MURDOCK

is in tremendous demand as one of the most dynamic speakers in America today.

More than 15,000 audiences in 39 countries have attended his Schools of Wisdom and conferences. Hundreds of invitations come to him from churches, colleges and business corporations. He is a noted author of over 200 books, including the best sellers, *The Leadership Secrets of Jesus* and *Secrets of the Richest Man Who Ever Lived*. Thousands view his weekly television program, *Wisdom Keys with Mike Murdock*. Many attend his Schools of Wisdom that he hosts in many cities of America.

☐ Yes, Mike! I made a decision to accept Christ as my personal Savior today. Please send me my free gift of your book, *31 Keys to a New Beginning* to help me with my new life in Christ. *(B-48)*

NAME _____ BIRTHDAY _____

ADDRESS _____

CITY _____ STATE ___ ZIP _____

PHONE _____ E-MAIL _____

Mail to: **The Wisdom Center** · 4051 Denton Hwy. · Ft. Worth, TX 76117
1-817-759-BOOK · 1-817-759-2665
You Will Love Our Website...! www.TheWisdomCenter.tv

Clip and Mail

JOIN THE
Wisdom Key 3000
TODAY!

Will You Become My Ministry Partner In The Work Of God?

Dear Friend,

God has connected us!

I have asked The Holy Spirit for 3000 Special Partners who will plant a monthly Seed of $58.00 to help me bring the gospel around the world. (58 represents 58 kinds of blessings in the Bible.)

Will you become my monthly Faith Partner in The Wisdom Key 3000? Your monthly Seed of $58.00 is so powerful in helping heal broken lives. When you sow into the work of God, 4 Miracle Harvests are guaranteed in Scripture, Isaiah 58...

- Uncommon Health (Isaiah 58)
- Uncommon Wisdom For Decision-Making (Isaiah 58)
- Uncommon Financial Favor (Isaiah 58)
- Uncommon Family Restoration (Isaiah 58)

Your Faith Partner,

Mike Murdock

P.S. Please clip the coupon attached and return it to me today, so I can rush the Wisdom Key Partnership Pak to you...or call me at 1-817-759-0300.

☐ *Yes Mike, I want to join The Wisdom Key 3000.*
Please rush The Wisdom Key Partnership Pak to me today!
☐ *Enclosed is my first monthly Seed-Faith Promise of:*
☐ *$58* ☐ *Other $_____.*

☐CHECK ☐MONEY ORDER ☐AMEX ☐DISCOVER ☐MASTERCARD ☐VISA

Credit Card # _____ Exp. ____/____

Signature _____

Name _____ Birth Date ____/____/____

Address _____

City _____ State _____ Zip _____

Phone _____ E-Mail _____

Your Seed-Faith offerings are used to support The Wisdom Center and all its programs. Your transaction may be electronically deposited. The Wisdom Center reserves the right to redirect funds as needed in order to carry out our charitable purpose.

THE WISDOM CENTER 4051 Denton Highway • Fort Worth, TX 76117 1-817-759-0300 1-817-759-2665

You Will Love Our Website:
www.TheWisdomCenter.tv

It Could Happen

Childless Couple Receives Baby Boy...!

In the fall, we planted a $58 Seed-Assignment to have a child. We had been told by 3 specialists that we couldn't have children. Nine months later I had a 9 lb. 4 oz. bouncing boy.

H.

Changes In Alzheimer's Disease...!

When you were at our church in Baltimore, in March of this year, I planted a $58 Seed for my mother's health and well-being. She will be 97 years old on May 27th and the doctor said Alzheimer's. We did not accept that diagnosis. About three weeks ago, we began to see and hear such a dramatic change in my mother that I know, and my family agrees, that God moved on her behalf. We expect her to have many more fruitful years.

B. - MD

Back Healed...!

I planted a $58 Seed when you were in San Diego last month. You told us to write "uncommon favor" on the check. First, I received a healing in my back that same Sunday! Then, yesterday I got news that they are putting a traffic signal at a very dangerous intersection on the way to work. I have been praying for that for many years!

B. - CA

Healing Is Harvest...!

Last February, I was waiting for a miracle. I planted a Seed of $116 in your ministry. I was put in the hospital. My doctor did a biopsy. It was cancer. I had thirty-six treatments plus two months of chemotherapy.

My doctor's report March 4, "...is without disease recurrence." Praise God.

J. - CA

To You!

Healing...!

My praise report is that I gave a $58 Seed and my health has been improving in my body. I asked you to pray for my lymphatic system and muscles that had broken down and shut down. Every day I feel strength in my legs I haven't felt before and I can tell the difference in my walk, and I am losing weight. I feel my strength coming back.　　　*C. G. - VA*

Leg Healed...!

The summer (June) I gave $58 love offering after reading "Covenant of 58 Blessings." I wrote in all four corners of my check what I needed from God. I had leg surgery in April, God saved my leg. Got 2 legs and 10 toes—all in good working condition.

My harvest so far: My leg is healed—no more pain or swelling. Somebody sent me $300 in the mail. My wife got blessed with favor with her boss.　　　*J. - TN*

Son Delivered From Drugs And Depression...!

I was impressed by the Lord to write a check out to you for $58.

Exactly thirteen days later my son, who was bound by drugs, alcohol and suffering from depression over the loss of his sister,...was totally and completely delivered from it all instantly. Now he's on a spiritual high with God! He said, "Mama, you've told me for eighteen years how good God really is, but I never really knew till now. "Praise God," he said.　　　*L. - SC*

Healing Of Chronic Depression...!

My sister, was healed from chronic depression after Seeding $58 to you for her.　　　*G. - NJ*

It Could Happen To You!

Income Increases And Parents Healed...!

The Holy Spirit moved me to sow two special $58 Seeds, and to believe God for 58 special blessings. I sowed a Seed for myself and wrote on the check, "Better Family and Life Relations." I sowed a Seed on behalf of my husband, and wrote on the check, "Better Family and Life Relations."

My husband found out that he had "unclaimed property" that had been turned into the State. The State of Texas sent him a check for over $1,100.

He got a tax refund check of over $8,000 delivered this week.

My dad, who had a stroke in December, has had his speech returned and he is up and can walk with a cane now. His mental facilities are intact and he is in good emotional condition.

My mother, who was in an auto accident, was told she needed surgery to correct the damage to her arm and shoulder joint. As of this week, the doctors are absolutely amazed at her progress. The woman is out using a chainsaw to cut down overgrown trees!

J & K. - TX

Pregnancy Miracle...!

The Lord spoke to me and told me to take one of my $58 per month Seeds...and sow it for her. Been praying three years for her to become pregnant. On 3/22 I sowed the Seed for her and told her to mark it as a memorial. On 5/28 she got her praise report, she is with child. Glory!!! Due date is 1/31.

M. - FL

Something Incredible Is Very Close To You.

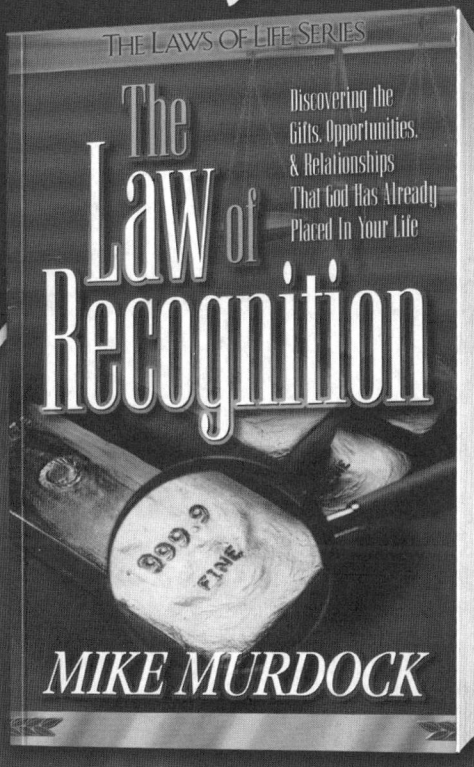

THE LAWS OF LIFE SERIES

The Law of Recognition

Discovering the Gifts, Opportunities, & Relationships That God Has Already Placed In Your Life

MIKE MURDOCK

- ▶ 47 Keys In Recognizing The Mate God Has Approved For You
- ▶ 14 Facts You Should Know About Your Gifts And Talents
- ▶ 17 Important Facts You Should Remember About Your Weakness
- ▶ 10 Wisdom Keys That Changed My Life
- ▶ 24 Powerful Facts About The Uncommon Dream Within You
- ▶ 6 Facts You Should Know About Managing Your Time
- ▶ 46 Important Facts You Should Know About Problem-Solving

Anything Unrecognized Becomes Uncelebrated. Anything Uncelebrated Becomes Unrewarded. Anything Unrewarded Eventually Exits Your Life. The Law of Recognition can turn a lifetime of failure into instant success. God has provided storehouses of treasures around us and we need only to recognize it. In this teaching you will learn to recognize the most important gifts in your life.

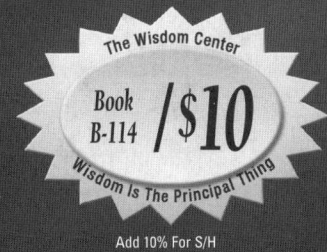

The Wisdom Center
Book B-114 / $10
Wisdom Is The Principal Thing

Add 10% For S/H

THE WISDOM CENTER 1-817-759-0300
4051 Denton Highway • Fort Worth TX, 76117 1-817-759-BOOK

You Will Love Our Website...!
TheWisdomCenter.tv

Learn From The Greatest.

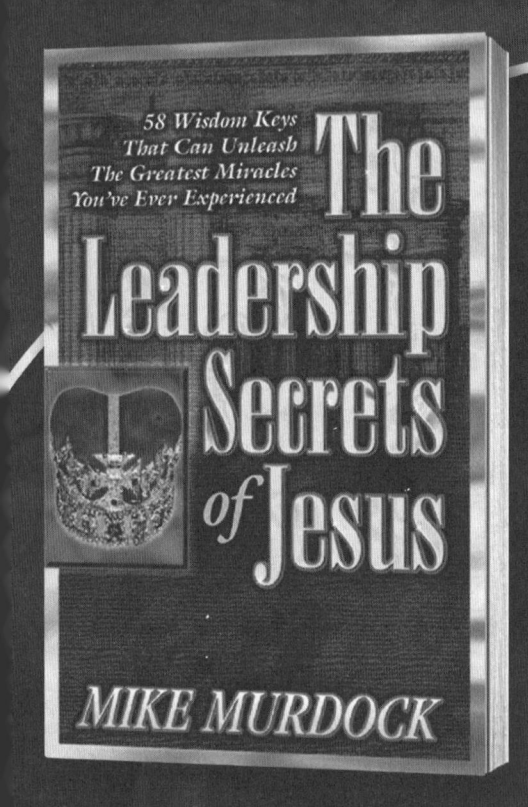

58 Wisdom Keys That Can Unleash The Greatest Miracles You've Ever Experienced

The Leadership Secrets of Jesus

MIKE MURDOCK

- ▶ The Secret Of Handling Rejection
- ▶ How To Deal With The Mistakes Of Others
- ▶ 5 Power Keys For Effective Delegation To Others
- ▶ The Key To Developing Great Faith
- ▶ The Greatest Qualities Of Champions
- ▶ The Secret Of The Wealthy
- ▶ 4 Goal-Setting Techniques
- ▶ 10 Facts Jesus Taught About Money

In this dynamic and practical guidebook Mike Murdock points you directly to Jesus, the Ultimate Mentor. You'll take just a moment every day to reflect on His life and actions. And when you do, you'll discover all the key skills and traits that Jesus used... the powerful "leadership secrets" that build true, lasting achievement. Explore them. Study them. Put them to work in your own life and your success will be assured!

The Wisdom Center
Book B-91 / $10
Wisdom Is The Principal Thing

Add 10% For S/H

THE WISDOM CENTER
4051 Denton Highway • Fort Worth TX, 76117
1-817-759-0300
1-817-759-BOOK

You Will Love Our Website...!
TheWisdomCenter.tv

My Gift Of Appreciation...
The Wisdom Commentary

The Wisdom Commentary includes 52 topics...for mentoring your family every week of the year.

These topics include:

- Abilities
- Achievement
- Anointing
- Assignment
- Bitterness
- Blessing
- Career
- Change
- Children
- Dating
- Depression
- Discipline
- Divorce
- Dreams And Goals
- Enemy
- Enthusiasm
- Favor
- Finances
- Fools
- Giving
- Goal-Setting
- God
- Happiness
- Holy Spirit
- Ideas
- Intercession
- Jobs
- Loneliness
- Love
- Mentorship
- Ministers
- Miracles
- Mistakes
- Money
- Negotiation
- Prayer
- Problem-Solving
- Protégés
- Satan
- Secret Place
- Seed-Faith
- Self-Confidence
- Struggle
- Success
- Time-Management
- Understanding
- Victory
- Weaknesses
- Wisdom
- Word Of God
- Words
- Work

Gift Of Appreciation For Your Sponsorship Seed of $100 or More

My Gift Of Appreciation To My Sponsors!...
Those Who Sponsor Two Square Feet In The Completion Of The Wisdom Center!

Thank you so much for becoming a part of this wonderful project...The completion of The Wisdom Center! The total purchase and renovation cost of this facility (135,000 square feet) is over $6,000,000. This is approximately $100 for every two square feet. **The Wisdom Commentary is my Gift of Appreciation for your Sponsorship Seed of $100...that sponsors two square feet of The Wisdom Center. Become a Sponsor!** You will love this Volume 1, of The Wisdom Commentary. It is my Gift of Appreciation for those who partner with me in the work of God.

Add 10% For S/H

THE WISDOM CENTER
4051 Denton Highway • Fort Worth TX, 76117
1-817-759-0300
1-817-759-BOOK

You Will Love Our Website...!
TheWisdomCenter.tv

CHAMPIONS 4
Book Pak!

① **Secrets of The Journey, Vol. 3** /Book (32pg/B-94/$5)
② **My Personal Dream Book**/Book (32pg/B-143/$5)
③ **Wisdom For Crisis Times** /Book (112pg/B-40/$9)
④ **The Making Of A Champion** /Book (128pg/B-59/$10)

The Wisdom Center
Champions 4 Book Pak!
Only $20
$29 Value
PAK-23
Wisdom Is The Principal Thing

*This offer expires December 31st, 2007. **Each Wisdom Book may be purchased separately if so desired.

Add 10% For S/H

THE WISDOM CENTER
4051 Denton Highway • Fort Worth, TX 76117
1-817-759-0300
1-817-759-BOOK

You Will Love Our Website...!
TheWisdomCenter.tv

80

The Businessman's Devotional 4 Book Pak!

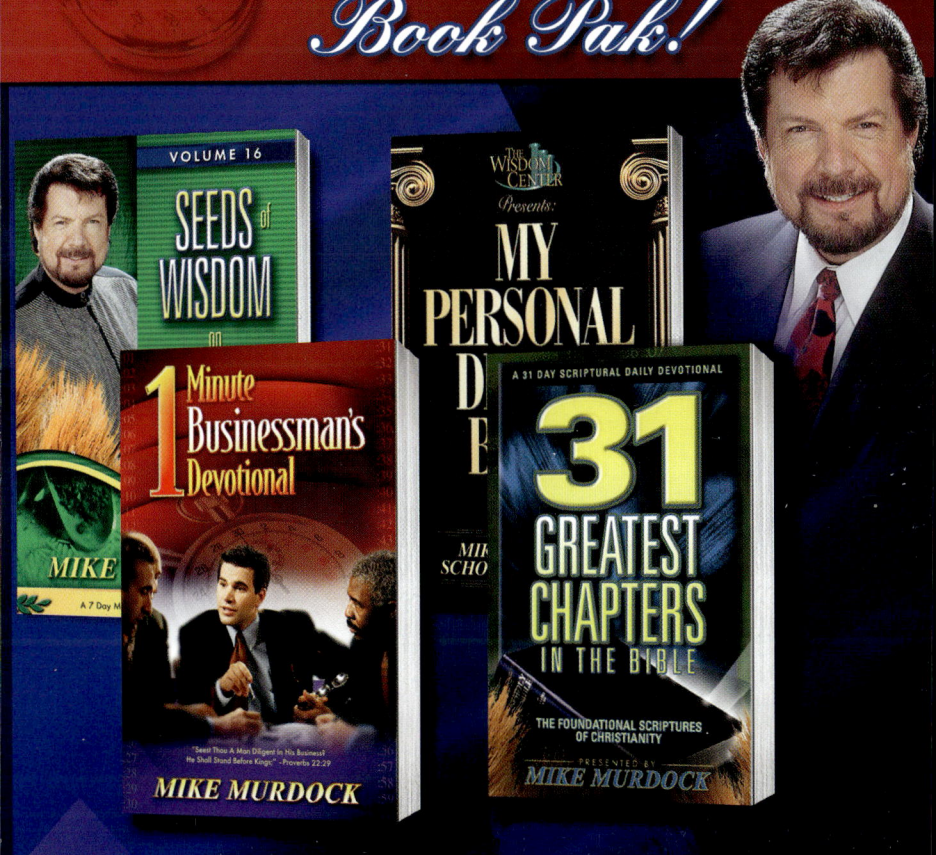

❶ **Seeds of Wisdom on Problem-Solving**/Book (32pg/B-118/$5)

❷ **My Personal Dream Book**/Book (32pg/B-143/$5)

❸ **1 Minute Businessman's Devotional**
/Book (224pg/B-42/$12)

❹ **31 Greatest Chapters In The Bible**
/Book (138pg/B-54/$10)

The Wisdom Center
The Businessman's Devotional 4 Book Pak!
Only $20 $32 Value
PAK-22
Wisdom Is The Principal Thing

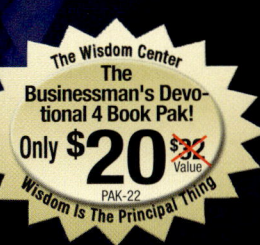

*Each Wisdom Book may be purchased separately if so desired.

Add 10% For S/H

THE WISDOM CENTER 1-817-759-BOOK
4051 Denton Highway • Fort Worth, TX 76117   1-817-759-0300

You Will Love Our Website...!
TheWisdomCenter.tv

A

The Businesswoman's Devotional Book Pak!

❶ **Seeds of Wisdom on Problem-Solving** /Book (32pg/B-118/$5)
❷ **My Personal Dream Book**/Book (32pg/B-143/$5)
❸ **1 Minute Businesswoman's Devotional**
   /Book (224pg/B-43/$12)
❹ **31 Greatest Chapters In The Bible**
   /Book (138pg/B-54/$10)

*Each Wisdom Book may be purchased separately if so desired.

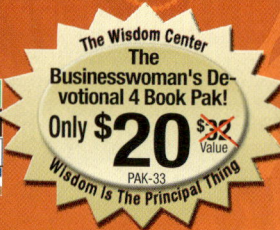

The Wisdom Center
The Businesswoman's Devotional 4 Book Pak!
Only $20
$32 Value
PAK-33
Wisdom Is The Principal Thing

Add 10% For S/H

THE WISDOM CENTER
4051 Denton Highway • Fort Worth, TX 76117
1-817-759-BOOK
1-817-759-0300

You Will Love Our Website...!
TheWisdomCenter.tv

Miracle 7 BOOK PAK!

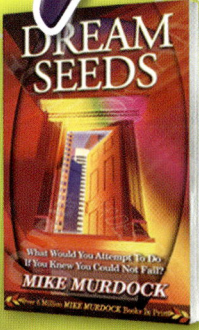

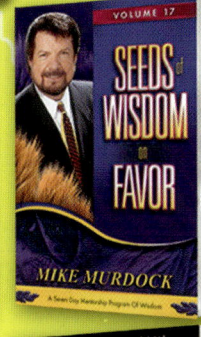

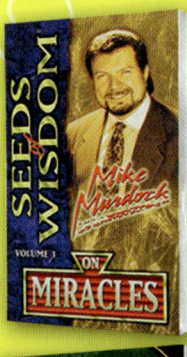

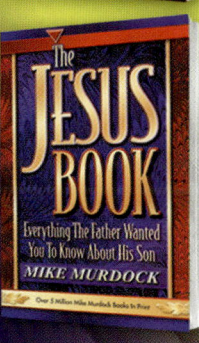

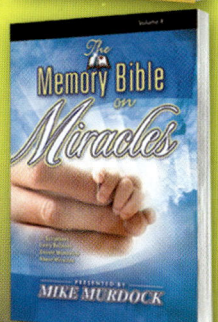

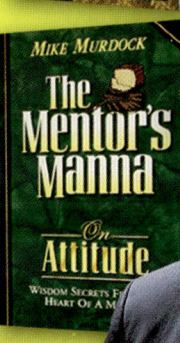

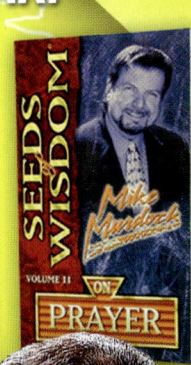

❶ **Dream Seeds**/Book (106pg/B-11/$9)

❷ **Seeds of Wisdom on Favor**/Book (32pg/B-119/$5)

❸ **Seeds of Wisdom on Miracles**/Book (32pg/B-15/$3)

❹ **Seeds of Wisdom on Prayer**/Book (32pg/B-23/$3)

❺ **The Jesus Book**/Book (166pg/B-27/$10)

❻ **The Memory Bible on Miracles**/Book (32pg/B-208/$3)

❼ **The Mentor's Manna on Attitude**/Book (32pg/B-58/$3)

DR. MIKE MURDOCK

The Wisdom Center
Miracle 7 Book Pak!
Only $30 — $36 Value
WBL-24
Wisdom Is The Principal Thing

Add 10% For S/H

Quantity Prices Available Upon Request

*Each Wisdom Book may be purchased separately if so desired.

THE WISDOM CENTER
4051 Denton Highway • Fort Worth, TX 76117
1-817-759-BOOK
1-817-759-0300

You Will Love Our Website...!
TheWisdomCenter.tv

Crisis 7 BOOK PAK!

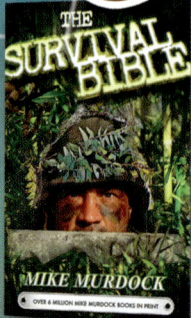

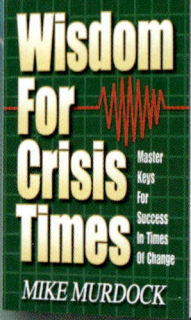

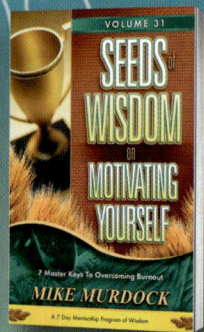

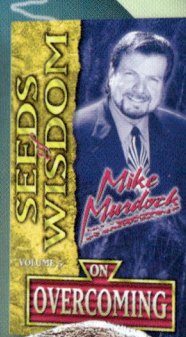

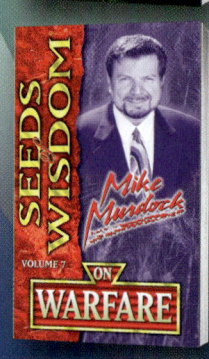

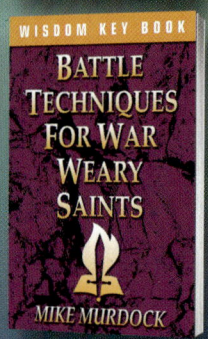

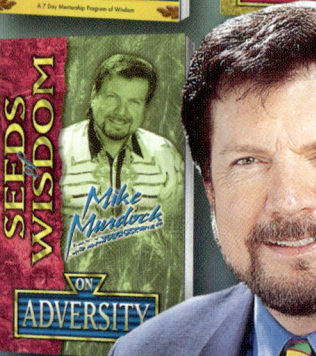

1. **The Survival Bible**/Book (248pg/B-29/$10)
2. **Wisdom For Crisis Times**/Book (112pg/B-40/$9)
3. **Seeds of Wisdom on Motivating Yourself**/Book (32pg/B-171/$5)
4. **Seeds of Wisdom on Overcoming**/Book (32pg/B-17/$3)
5. **Seeds of Wisdom on Warfare**/Book (32pg/B-19/$3)
6. **Battle Techniques For War-Weary Saints**/Book (32pg/B-07/$5)
7. **Seeds of Wisdom on Adversity**/Book (32pg/B-21/$3)

*Each Wisdom Book may be purchased separately if so desired.

DR. MIKE MURDOCK

The Wisdom Center
Crisis 7 Book Pak!
Only $30 $36 Value
WBL-25
Wisdom Is The Principal Thing

Add 10% For S/H
Quantity Prices Available Upon Request

THE WISDOM CENTER
4051 Denton Highway • Fort Worth, TX 76117
1-817-759-BOOK
1-817-759-0300
You Will Love Our Website...!
TheWisdomCenter.tv

Money 7 BOOK PAK!

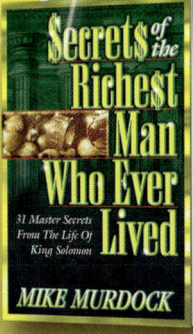

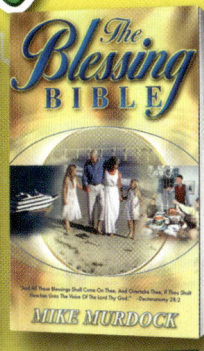

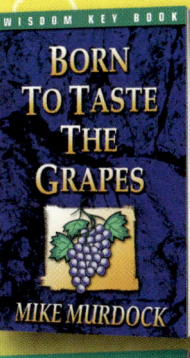

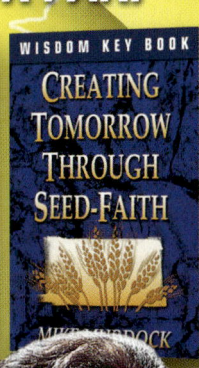

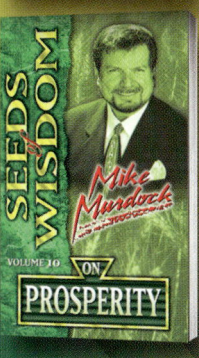

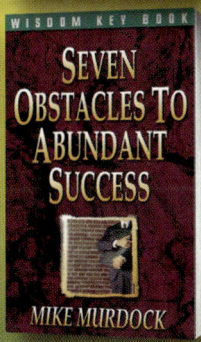

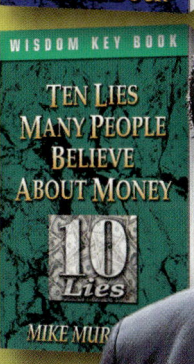

1. **Secrets of the Richest Man Who Ever Lived**/Book (179pg/B-99/$10)
2. **The Blessing Bible**/Book (252pg/B-28/$10)
3. **Born To Taste The Grapes**/Book (32pg/B-65/$3)
4. **Creating Tomorrow Through Seed-Faith**/Book (32pg/B-06/$5)
5. **Seeds of Wisdom on Prosperity**/Book (32pg/B-22/$3)
6. **Seven Obstacles To Abundant Success**/Book (32pg/B-64/$3)
7. **Ten Lies Many People Believe About Money**/Book (32pg/B-04/$5)

*Each Wisdom Book may be purchased separately if so desired.

The Wisdom Center
Money 7 Book Pak!
Only $30 $39 Value
WBL-30
Wisdom Is The Principal Thing

Add 10% For S/H

DR. MIKE MURDOCK

THE WISDOM CENTER
4051 Denton Highway • Fort Worth, TX 76117
1-817-759-BOOK
1-817-759-0300

You Will Love Our Website...!
TheWisdomCenter.tv

E

Career 7
Book Pak For Business People!

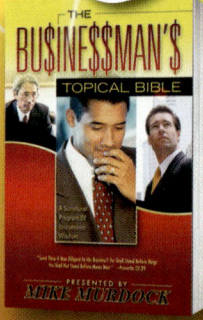

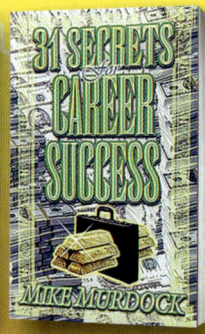

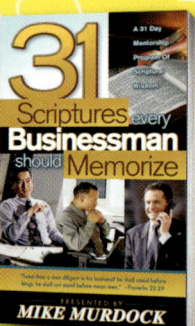

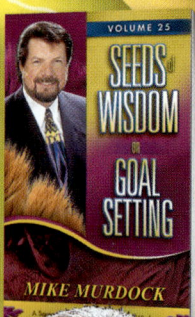

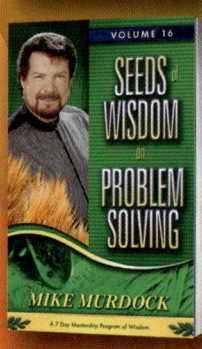

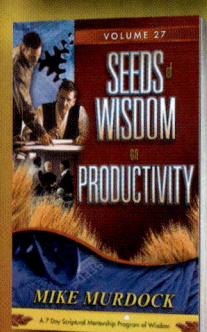

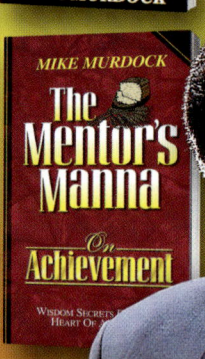

① **The Businessman's Topical Bible**/Book (384pg/B-33/$10)

② **31 Secrets for Career Success**/Book (114pg/B-44/$10)

③ **31 Scriptures Every Businessman Should Memorize**/Book (32pg/B-141/$3)

④ **Seeds of Wisdom on Goal-Setting**/Book (32pg/B-127/$5)

⑤ **Seeds of Wisdom on Problem-Solving**/Book (32pg/B-118/$5)

⑥ **Seeds of Wisdom on Productivity**/Book (32pg/B-137/$5)

⑦ **The Mentor's Manna on Achievement**/Book (32pg/B-79/$3)

*Each Wisdom Book may be purchased separately if so desired.

DR. MIKE MURDOCK

The Wisdom Center
Career 7 Book Pak!
Only $30
$41 Value
WBL-27
Wisdom Is The Principal Thing

Add 10% For S/H

THE WISDOM CENTER
4051 Denton Highway • Fort Worth, TX 76117
1-817-759-BOOK
1-817-759-0300

You Will Love Our Website...!
TheWisdomCenter.tv

Spirit Music.

TS-59

Free Book ENCLOSED!
B-100 ($10 Value)

Songs...

1. A Holy Place
2. Anything You Want
3. Everything Comes From You
4. Fill This Place With Your Presence
5. First Thing Every Morning
6. Holy Spirit, I Want To Hear You
7. Holy Spirit, Move Again
8. Holy Spirit, You Are Enough
9. I Don't Know What I Would Do Without You
10. I Let Go (Of Anything That Stops Me)
11. I'll Just Fall On You
12. I Love You, Holy Spirit
13. I'm Building My Life Around You
14. I'm Giving Myself To You
15. I'm In Love! I'm In Love!
16. I Need Water (Holy Spirit, You're My Well)
17. In The Secret Place
18. In Your Presence, I'm Always Changed
19. In Your Presence (Miracles Are Born)
20. I've Got To Live In Your Presence
21. I Want To Hear Your Voice
22. I Will Do Things Your Way
23. Just One Day At A Time
24. Meet Me In The Secret Place
25. More Than Ever Before
26. Nobody Else Does What You Do
27. No No Walls!
28. Nothing Else Matters Anymore (Since I've Been In The Presence Of You Lord)
29. Nowhere Else
30. Once Again You've Answered
31. Only A Fool Would Try (To Live Without You)
32. Take Me Now
33. Teach Me How To Please You
34. There's No Place I'd Rather Be
35. Thy Word Is All That Matters
36. When I Get In Your Presence
37. You're The Best Thing (That's Ever Happened To Me)
38. You Are Wonderful
39. You've Done It Once
40. You Keep Changing Me
41. You Satisfy

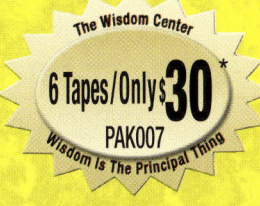

6 Tapes / Only $30*
PAK007

Add 10% For S/H

THE WISDOM CENTER
4051 Denton Highway • Fort Worth, TX 76117
1-817-759-BOOK
1-817-759-0300

You Will Love Our Website...!
TheWisdomCenter.tv

G

YOUR ASSIGNMENT IS YOUR DISTINCTION FROM OTHERS.

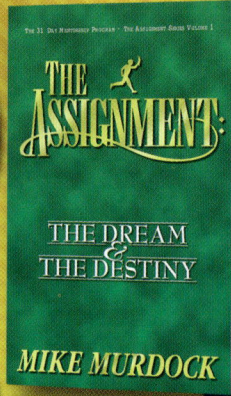

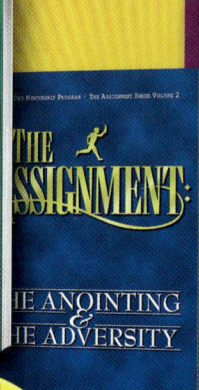

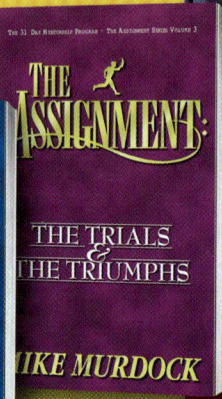

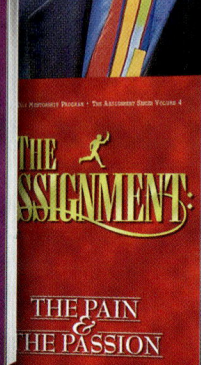

Assignment 4 Book Pak!

Uncommon Wisdom For Discovering Your Life Assignment.

1. **The Dream & The Destiny**
   Vol 1/Book (164 pg/B-74/$10)
2. **The Anointing & The Adversity**
   Vol 2/Book (192 pg/B-75/$10)
3. **The Trials & The Triumphs**
   Vol 3/Book (160 pg/B-97/$10)
4. **The Pain & The Passion**
   Vol 4/Book (144 pg/B-98/$10)

*Each Wisdom Book may be purchased separately if so desired.

Buy 3 Books & Get The 4th Book Free!

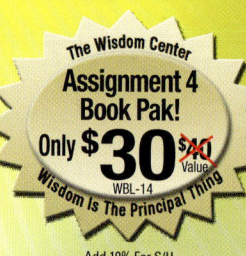

The Wisdom Center
Assignment 4 Book Pak!
Only $30 $40 Value
WBL-14
Wisdom Is The Principal Thing

Add 10% For S/H

THE WISDOM CENTER
4051 Denton Highway • Fort Worth, TX 76117
1-817-759-BOOK
1-817-759-0300

You Will Love Our Website...!
TheWisdomCenter.tv

101 Wisdom Keys That Have Most Changed My Life.

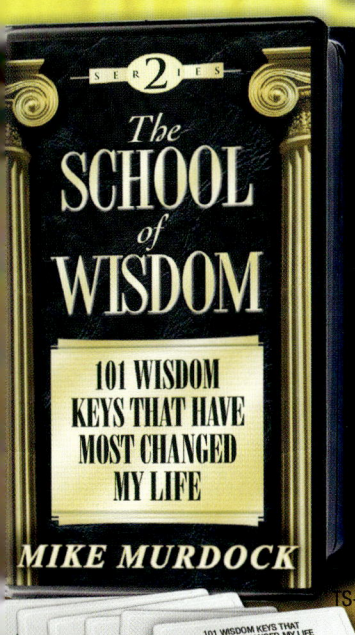

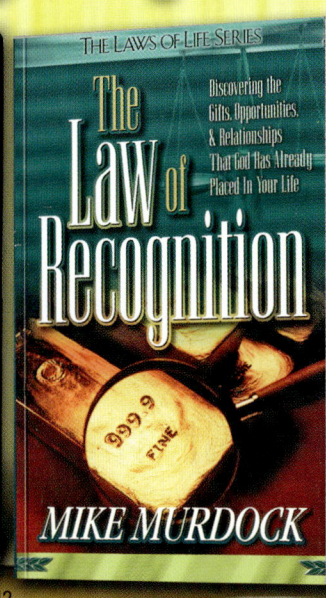

School of Wisdom #2 Pak!

- What Attracts Others Toward You
- The Secret Of Multiplying Your Financial Blessings
- What Stops The Flow Of Your Faith
- Why Some Fail And Others Succeed
- How To Discern Your Life Assignment
- How To Create Currents Of Favor With Others
- How To Defeat Loneliness
- 47 Keys In Recognizing The Mate God Has Approved For You
- 14 Facts You Should Know About Your Gifts And Talents
- 17 Important Facts You Should Remember About Your Weakness
- And Much, Much More...

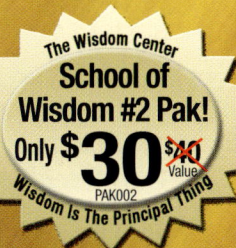

The Wisdom Center
School of Wisdom #2 Pak!
Only $30 $40 Value
PAK002
Wisdom Is The Principal Thing

Add 10% For S/H

THE WISDOM CENTER
4051 Denton Highway • Fort Worth, TX 76117
1-817-759-BOOK
1-817-759-0300

You Will Love Our Website...!
TheWisdomCenter.tv

Financial $ecrets.

The Wisdom Center
Buy One...
Receive The
Second One
FREE!
Wisdom Is The Principal Thing

31 REAON PEOPLE DO NOT RECEIVE THEIR FINANCIAL HARVE$T
THE 31 DAY MENTORSHIP PROGRAM
MIKE MURDOCK

7 KEYS to 1000 TIMES MORE
VIDEO
The Lord God Of Your Fathers Make You A Thousand Times So Many More As You Are, And Bless You, As He Hath Promised You!
Deuteronomy 1:11
MIKE MURDOCK

Your Financial World Will Change Forever.

Video 2-Pak!

▸ 8 Scriptural Reasons You Should Pursue Financial Prosperity

▸ The Secret Prayer Key You Need When Making A Financial Request To God

▸ The Weapon Of Expectation And The 5 Miracles It Unlocks

▸ How To Discern Those Who Qualify To Receive Your Financial Assistance

▸ How To Predict The Miracle Moment God Will Schedule Your Financial Breakthrough

▸ Habits Of Uncommon Achievers

▸ The Greatest Success Law I Ever Discovered

▸ How To Discern Your Place Of Assignment, The Only Place Financial Provision Is Guaranteed

▸ 3 Secret Keys In Solving Problems For Others

The Wisdom Center
Video 2-Pak!
Only $30 $60 Value
VIPAK-01
Wisdom Is The Principal Thing

Add 10% For S/H

THE WISDOM CENTER
4051 Denton Highway • Fort Worth, TX 76117
1-817-759-BOOK
1-817-759-0300

You Will Love Our Website...!
TheWisdomCenter.tv

Favor 4!

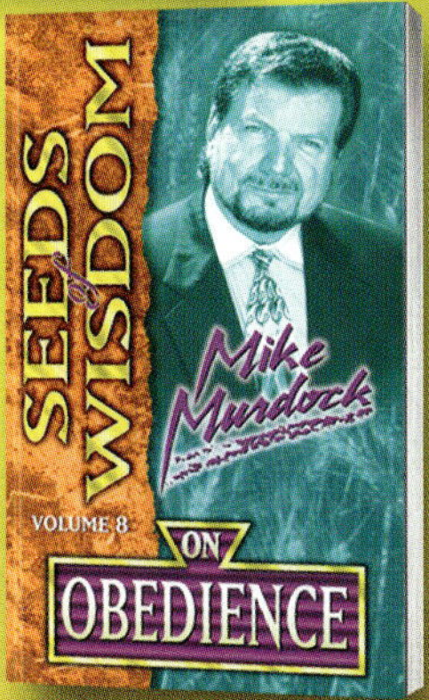

This Collection Of Wisdom Will Change The Seasons Of Your Life Forever!

❶ **The School of Wisdom #4 / 31 Keys To Unleashing Uncommon Favor...Tape Series**/6 Cassettes (TS-44/$30)

❷ **The Hidden Power Of Right Words...**
The Wisdom Center Pastoral Library/CD (WCPL-27/$10)

❸ **Seeds of Wisdom on Favor**/Book (32pg/B-119/$5)

❹ **Seeds of Wisdom on Obedience**/Book (32pg/B-20/$3)

*Each Wisdom Product may be purchased separately if so desired.

The Wisdom Center
Favor 4 Collection!
Only $35 $48 Value
PAK-12
Wisdom Is The Principal Thing

Add 10% For S/H

THE WISDOM CENTER
4051 Denton Highway • Fort Worth, TX 76117
1-817-759-BOOK
1-817-759-0300

You Will Love Our Website...!
TheWisdomCenter.tv

K

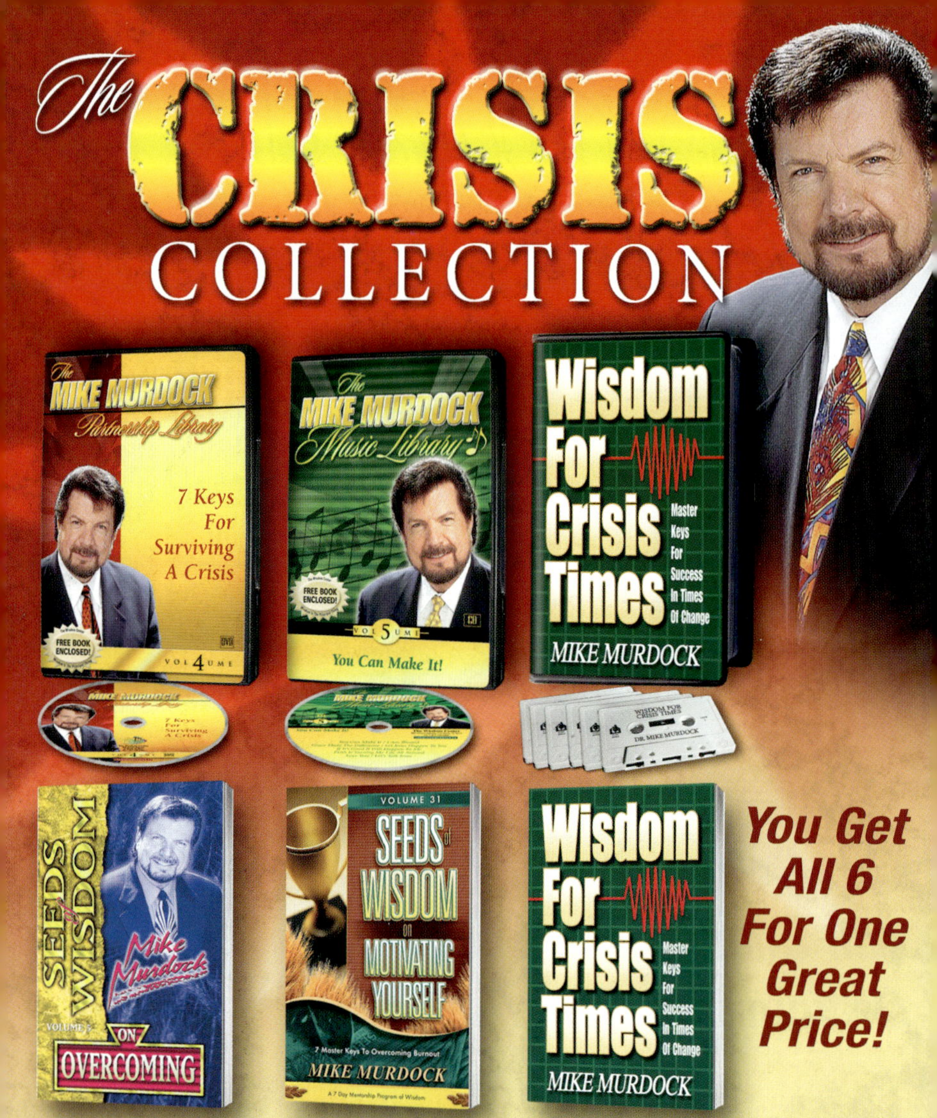

The CRISIS COLLECTION

You Get All 6 For One Great Price!

❶ 7 Keys For Surviving A Crisis/DVD (MMPL-04D/$10)
❷ You Can Make It!/Music CD (MMML-05/$10)
❸ Wisdom For Crisis Times/6 Cassettes (TS-40/$30)
❹ Seeds of Wisdom on Overcoming/Book (32pg/B-17/$3)
❺ Seeds of Wisdom on Motivating Yourself/Book (32pg/B-171/$5)
❻ Wisdom For Crisis Times/Book (112pg/B-40/$9)

Also Included... Two Free Bonus Books!

*Each Wisdom Product may be purchased separately if so desired.

The Wisdom Center
The Crisis Collection Only $40 $67 Value
PAK-16
Wisdom Is The Principal Thing

Add 10% For S/H

THE WISDOM CENTER
4051 Denton Highway • Fort Worth, TX 76117
1-817-759-BOOK
1-817-759-0300

You Will Love Our Website...!
TheWisdomCenter.tv

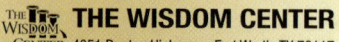

THE TURNAROUND Collection

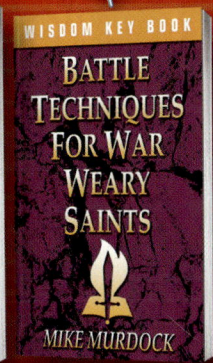

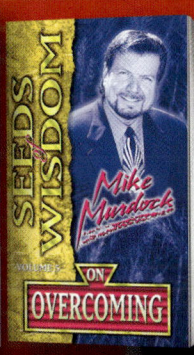

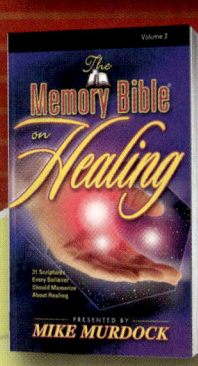

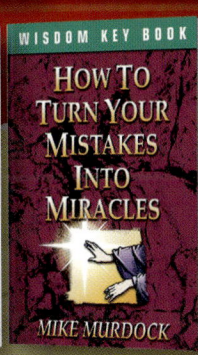

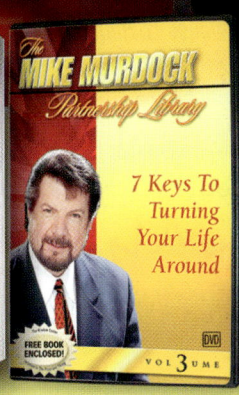

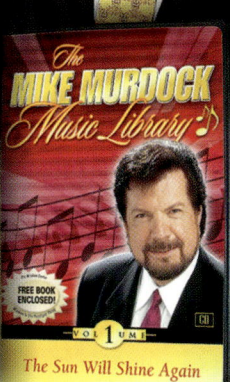

1. **The Wisdom Commentary Vol. 1**/Book (256pg/52 Topics/B-136/$20)
2. **Battle Techniques For War-Weary Saints**/Book (32pg/B-07/$5)
3. **Seeds of Wisdom on Overcoming**/Book (32pg/B-17/$3)
4. **The Memory Bible on Healing**/Book (32pg/B-196/$3)
5. **How To Turn Your Mistakes Into Miracles**/Book (32pg/B-56/$5)
6. **7 Keys To Turning Your Life Around**/DVD (MMPL-03D/$10)
7. **The Sun Will Shine Again**/Music CD (MMML-01/$10)

*Each Wisdom Product may be purchased separately if so desired.

The Wisdom Center
The Turnaround Collection Only $40 $56 Value
PAK-15
Wisdom Is The Principal Thing

Add 10% For S/H

THE WISDOM CENTER
4051 Denton Highway • Fort Worth, TX 76117
1-817-759-BOOK
1-817-759-0300

You Will Love Our Website...!
TheWisdomCenter.tv

M

THE WISDOM BIBLE
Partnership Edition

Over 120 Wisdom Study Guides Included Such As:

- 10 Qualities Of Uncommon Achievers
- 18 Facts You Should Know About The Anointing
- 21 Facts To Help You Identify Those Assigned To You
- 31 Facts You Should Know About Your Assignment
- 8 Keys That Unlock Victory In Every Attack
- 22 Defense Techniques To Remember During Seasons Of Personal Attack
- 20 Wisdom Keys And Techniques To Remember During An Uncommon Battle
- 11 Benefits You Can Expect From God
- 31 Facts You Should Know About Favor
- The Covenant Of 58 Blessings
- 7 Keys To Receiving Your Miracle
- 16 Facts You Should Remember About Contentious People
- 5 Facts Solomon Taught About Contracts
- 7 Facts You Should Know About Conflict
- 6 Steps That Can Unlock Your Self-Confidence
- And Much More!

Your Partnership makes such a difference in The Wisdom Center Outreach Ministries. I wanted to place a Gift in your hand that could last a lifetime for you and your family...**The Wisdom Study Bible.**

40 Years of Personal Notes...this Partnership Edition Bible contains 160 pages of my Personal Study Notes...that could forever change your Bible Study of The Word of God. This **Partnership Edition...**is my personal **Gift of Appreciation** when you sow your Sponsorship Seed of $1,000 to help us complete The Prayer Center and TV Studio Complex. An Uncommon Seed Always Creates An Uncommon Harvest!

Mike

Thank you from my heart for your Seed of Obedience (Luke 6:38).

THE WISDOM CENTER
4051 Denton Highway • Fort Worth, TX 76117
1-817-759-BOOK
1-817-759-0300
You Will Love Our Website...!
TheWisdomCenter.tv

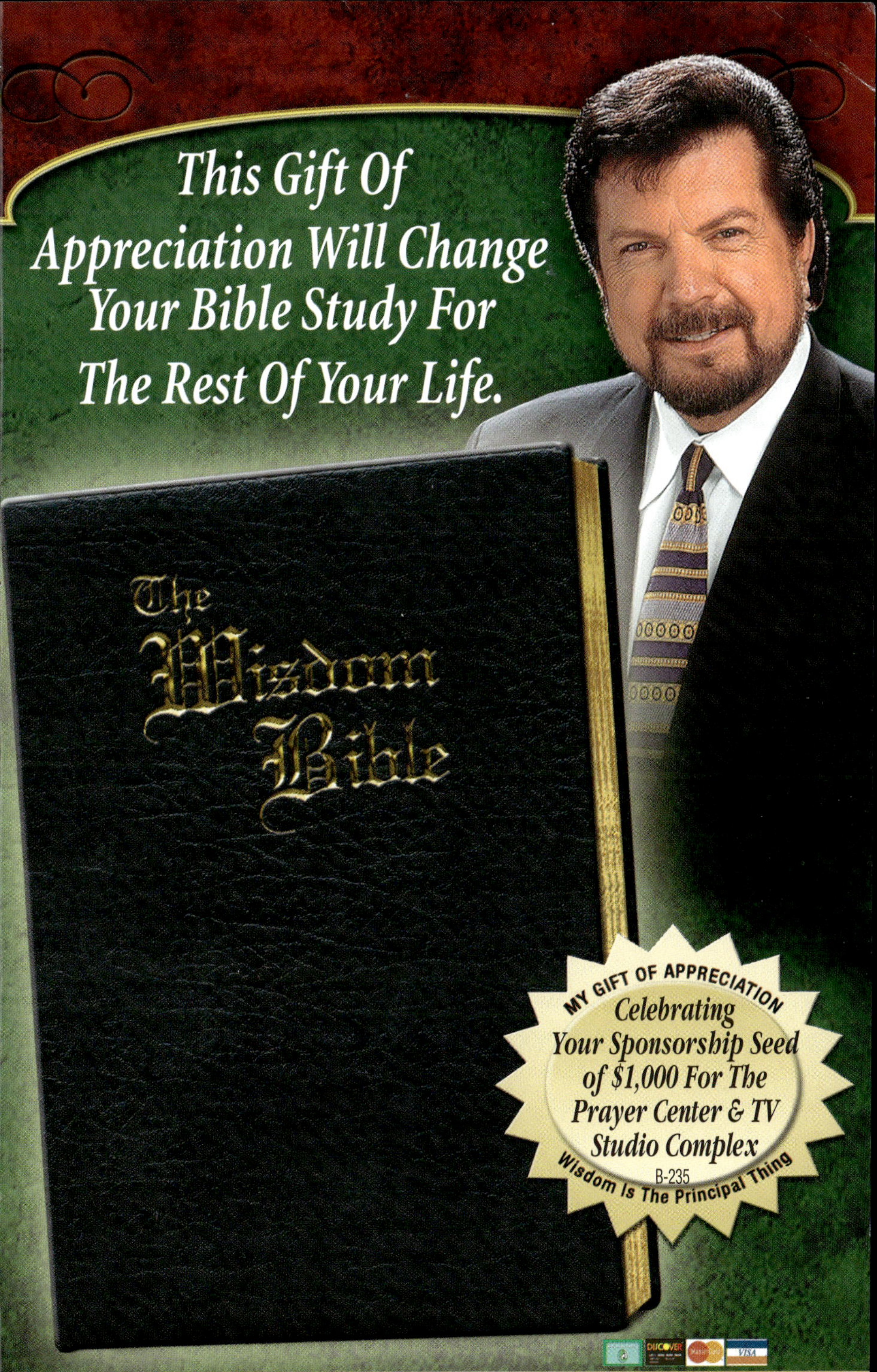

This Gift Of Appreciation Will Change Your Bible Study For The Rest Of Your Life.

The Wisdom Bible

MY GIFT OF APPRECIATION
Celebrating Your Sponsorship Seed of $1,000 For The Prayer Center & TV Studio Complex
B-235
Wisdom Is The Principal Thing

THE WISDOM CENTER 1-817-759-BOOK
4051 Denton Highway • Fort Worth, TX 76117   1-817-759-0300

You Will Love Our Website...!
TheWisdomCenter.tv   O

JOIN THE
Wisdom Key 3000
TODAY!

Will You Become My Ministry Partner In The Work Of God?

Dear Friend,

God has connected us!

I have asked The Holy Spirit for 3000 Special Partners who will plant a monthly Seed of $58.00 to help me bring the gospel around the world. (58 represents 58 kinds of blessings in the Bible.)

Will you become my monthly Faith Partner in The Wisdom Key 3000? Your monthly Seed of $58.00 is so powerful in helping heal broken lives. When you sow into the work of God, 4 Miracle Harvests are guaranteed in Scripture, Isaiah 58...

- ▶ Uncommon Health (Isaiah 58)
- ▶ Uncommon Wisdom For Decision-Making (Isaiah 58)
- ▶ Uncommon Financial Favor (Isaiah 58)
- ▶ Uncommon Family Restoration (Isaiah 58)

Your Faith Partner,

Mike Murdock

P.S. Please clip the coupon attached and return it to me today, so I can rush the Wisdom Key Partnership Pak to you...or call me at 1-817-759-0300.

PP-03

☐ **Yes Mike, I want to join The Wisdom Key 3000. Please rush The Wisdom Key Partnership Pak to me today!**

☐ **Enclosed is my first monthly Seed-Faith Promise of:**
☐ **$58** ☐ **Other $_____.**

☐ CHECK ☐ MONEY ORDER ☐ AMEX ☐ DISCOVER ☐ MASTERCARD ☐ VISA

Credit Card # _____ Exp. ____/____

Signature _____

Name _____ Birth Date ____/____

Address _____

City _____ State _____ Zip _____

Phone _____ E-Mail _____

Your Seed-Faith offerings are used to support The Wisdom Center and all its programs. Your transaction may be electronically deposited. The Wisdom Center reserves the right to redirect funds as needed in order to carry out our charitable purpose.

THE WISDOM CENTER 1-817-759-BOOK
4051 Denton Highway • Fort Worth, TX 76117   1-817-759-0300

You Will Love Our Website...!
TheWisdomCenter.tv